ENERGY IN ACTION

The Power of Emotions
and Intuition to Cultivate
Peace and Freedom

SHERIANNA BOYLE

sounds true
BOULDER, COLORADO

Sounds True
Boulder, CO 80306

Published 2023

Cover design by Jennifer Miles

Book design by Meredith Jarrett

Printed in Canada

BK06567

Library of Congress Cataloging-in-Publication Data

Names: Boyle, Sherianna, author.
Title: Energy in action : the power of emotions and intuition to cultivate peace
and freedom / Sherianna Boyle, MEd, CAGS.
Description: Boulder, CO : Sounds True, [2023]
Identifiers: LCCN 2022041160 (print) | LCCN 2022041161 (ebook) | ISBN
9781649630261 (paperback) | ISBN 9781649630278 (ebook)
Subjects: LCSH: Emotions. | Intuition.
Classification: LCC BF511 .B69 2023 (print) | LCC BF511
(ebook) | DDC 152.4—dc23/eng/20221116
LC record available at https://lccn.loc.gov/2022041160
LC ebook record available at https://lccn.loc.gov/2022041161

FSC
www.fsc.org
MIX
Paper from
responsible sources
FSC® C016245

10 9 8 7 6 5 4 3 2 1

PRAISE FOR *ENERGY IN ACTION*

"Change your energetic frequency, change your life! This book is practical, profound, and life altering."

ELIZABETH GUARINO
author of *The Change Guidebook*

"Sherianna has created an incredible system for healing, cleansing, and raising your vibration. Her work is colorful, light, and inspiring. Highly recommend!"

AMY LEIGH MERCREE
medical intuitive and bestselling author of 16 books, including *The Healing Home: A Room-by-Room Guide to Positive Vibes*

"Sherianna has the heart of a healer. Her work empowers people to release pain and suffering and live with more intention, joy, and ease. This book gives practical tools and provides a clear road map for helping to clear fear so you can help connect more deeply to your true self and others."

SHANNON KAISER
bestselling author of *The Self-Love Experiment* and *Return to You*

"Balancing spirituality and psychology, *Energy in Action* is the go-to guide for conscious, soul-driven manifestation. Sherianna has a talent for explaining complex spiritual concepts in simple ways and teaching practical ways of working with energy. Centered around Universal laws, this book goes beyond simplistic explanations of manifestation and provides a holistic guidebook to co-creating your life and purpose."

GEORGE LIZOS
psychic healer and bestselling author of *Protect Your Light*

"The material in this book is totally unique to open the door to our own internal clarity and let go of past thoughts holding us back. I believe you will find this book enjoyable as you read pages offering altered perceptions that allow for a wonderful spirit of personal transformation!"

BERNIE ASHMAN
astrologer and author of *Sun Sign Karma*

"Through her own soul growth, Sherianna guides us to new revelations of how we can build spiritual confidence when processing our feelings and emotions. We learn we may have unknowingly been disrupting the flow when visualizing what we want to manifest. She shares: 'You don't desire what you haven't already experienced on an energetic level.' Blending the insights of The Spiritual Laws of the Universe, Sherianna's *Energy in Action* gives the reader a clear path to peace within, harmony, and actualizing manifestations."

DEBORAH BEAUVAIS
founder of Dreamvisions 7 Radio Network

ALSO BY SHERIANNA BOYLE

Emotional Detox Card Deck

Emotional Detox: 7 Steps to Release Toxicity & Energize Joy

Emotional Detox for Anxiety

*Emotional Detox Now: 135 Self-Guided Practices
to Renew Your Mind, Heart & Spirit*

Mantras Made Easy

The Four Gifts of Anxiety

*Choosing Love: Discover How to Connect
to the Universal Power of Love*

The Conscious Parent's Guide to Childhood Anxiety

The Everything Parent's Guide to Childhood Anxiety

Powered by Me for Educators

"Nothing happens until something moves."
ALBERT EINSTEIN

Contents

The Thirteen Rays of Light

My friends, we are ascending into a new time. Old ways of functioning (ego and control) are loosening, to be replaced by higher states of consciousness. With this comes an intuitive awakening of your manifesting potential. The rays of light are here to help; soon you will see.

Here is a list of the rays of light we will be working with. A free colored chart can be found at sheriannaboyle.com.

Diamond
White
Yellow
Pink
Orange
Blue
Magenta
Red or Ruby
Green
Silver
Indigo
Violet
Gold

Dear Reader

There are two things I think you ought to know about the Spiritual Laws of the Universe. The first is they are a guidance system for moving energy. The second is once the energy is in motion within you, they reflect you in your purest and highest form.

This is the state you want to manifest from.

To understand, think of it like this. If you wanted to get better reception on your phone or computer, you would be inclined to move to a location with a stronger signal. If that did not work, you might purchase a device to amplify your reception. This is similar to how the Laws of the Universe work: they can raise your vibration, boosting your energetic signal.

Yet, up 'til now, many of the teachings around manifesting have been focused on changing your thoughts. While choosing to manifest in this way is not wrong or bad, it can feel much like having a weak signal. At some point, you may wonder if the universe is hearing you at all.

You see, focusing on thoughts is like reading an old newspaper. By the time whatever you are experiencing has translated into a thought form, the energy has been diluted. Emotions and intuition, on the other hand, are energy generators. When you allow them to exist, they can elevate your consciousness, strengthening your inner energy signal.

It is not a matter of *what* or *how* you create, but *where*—the quality of inner space from which you generate manifestations—you bring something conceptual into the physical.

Think of it this way: If you were to sit down at a table stacked with books, papers, and stained coffee cups and I asked you to create something, you might think there is no room to produce anything there. If I asked you to remove the objects, you may find yourself overwhelmed or frustrated with the process. This is because some items (for example, unpaid bills) may be emotionally triggering. Having these attachments and triggers can clog up your intuition and connection to the Spiritual Laws of the Universe.

Here is the good news: once you learn how to approach your emotions in this way, your tendency to distract from what you feel will decrease. Instead, you will turn to energy in action as a resource for inner strength, peace, calm, clarity, abundance, and more.

Emotions and intuition go hand in hand. Block one (for example, emotions) and you will inevitably clog up the other (intuition). Keeping your energy field open, aligned, and connected is key to the process. At the same time, you are both a human and a soul; therefore, you have history. For that reason, you may have developed ways of functioning that keep your guard up, shut down your energy, and stifle your intuition. Trust that your soul remembers just how powerful you are, and the system I created to help you detox those patterns, which I call the Cleanse, provides a pathway for accessing this higher wisdom.

After doing the Cleanse practice on my own, I discovered that it can help people through tough moments, triggers, and habits with effortlessness and ease. As a result, new teachings (ones I never heard before) around the Spiritual Laws of the Universe also arrived.

This book may be different from other ones you've read because here, not only will you be sharpening your manifesting skills while learning about the Spiritual Laws of the Universe, but you will also be doing it in a way that supports the development of the greater good for others and the planet. You see, I believe manifesting was never meant to be a "me" practice, but rather it is a "we" practice. The Spiritual Laws reinforce this, which you'll soon see. Through this process, you are going to be able to create what you desire in a whole new way. As you develop your skills, you will find yourself less interested in things like negativity, drama, or fear that pull you off course.

For far too long, we have been taught to manifest from a place of desperation, fear, and brokenness. When we're worried about money, we are told it is because we focus too much on scarcity; when we're tired of being alone, we are told it is because we aren't imagining life with another person. That's where the mindset of energy in action comes in handy. It helps you shift attention from what you *want* to transforming what you *feel*.

Feeling is what ignites your intuition, and when these two (emotions and intuition) open, your life will become more fluid. Rather than get stuck in patterns, you will move through them like running water. This is energy in action.

Many people confuse goal setting with intention setting. To help you, I developed a simple way to look at it: the goal is what you are aiming for, but your intention is the energy in action that will help propel you toward reaching that goal.

○ If you want to increase something, like love, finances, health, balance, or happiness, then your intention would be to *allow* and *receive*.

○ If you want to decrease something, like anxiety, fear, insecurity, conflict, or self-destructive behavior, then your intention would be to *notice* and *observe*.

What are you *allowing, receiving, noticing, and observing*? What is it like to shift from focusing on what you want to having enough energy to both see and trust what you have? This includes the powerful vibrations that are available to you right now, in this very moment. Yet if your mind is preoccupied with fearful thoughts and the energy around your heart is hardened by past events, you may miss the opportunity and inadvertently choose to rerun old patterns.

Let's face it, the number of negative influences on you (such as social media, political discord, and environmental shifts) today is enormous. These influences affect the way you see and interact with the world around you. When these influences take energy away from you (as many of them do), your manifesting potential can be diluted by fear, insecurity, anxiety, self-doubt, and more. As you learn to Cleanse toxicity and tune in to powerful vibrations of unconditional love, freedom, and peace, your manifesting abilities begin to explode, simply because you are being the best version of you.

Not only will you be able to manifest the life you desire, but you'll also be manifesting the amplification of a new earth energy. It is your inner movement of energy that can transform fear and control into peace and freedom.

With love,

Sherianna

Introduction

Our emotions were never meant to be contained or managed; they are meant to be felt. Through the integration of psychology, mindfulness, and tools for increasing self-awareness, you can learn to move the energy of both conscious and subconscious emotions to amplify your creative potential.

You may be wondering if you are even cut out for all this manifesting stuff. Maybe you took a shot at it several years ago when the book (and eventually the movie) *The Secret* came out. I mean, who wouldn't want to will their dreams and desires into reality? After all, the basic idea of the Law of Attraction makes intuitive sense: *positive or negative thoughts bring positive or negative experiences.* Maybe you went all-in and poured your heart and soul into creating a vision board, eager to see the words and images come to fruition, but then . . . nothing. If so, I totally get it. I too wanted to believe that if I visualized something long enough, pictured myself as already having it in my life, it would eventually happen . . . but it doesn't work that way, does it?

What I didn't consider when I was trying to think my way into what I wanted were my emotions.

I eventually discovered that if we control or suppress our emotions instead of moving them, manifesting won't happen, at least not in the way we hoped it would. Instead, emotions become an obstacle. If your emotions are left motionless, the energy inside you can become tight or constricted. When this happens, you are more likely to react *to* rather than move *through* what you feel. This can be troubling because in order to manifest the life you desire, your emotions must be in motion. Here is the thing: the opposite of reaction is action, which is how I came to define manifesting as *energy in action.*

Yet, most of us have learned to focus on the outside first. Rather than go inward, far too often we rely on our external physical world—distractions, like our phones, or comforts, like food or alcohol—to help us manage what we feel inside. While living your life from the outside-in may make you feel like you have things in control—from everyday details to potential catastrophes—you have to wonder, what is the *quality* of energy you are putting into your actions?

So, often without realizing it, in order to control, contain, or prevent your feelings, you may be putting into motion a management system instead of a movement system. As a result, all that managing of emotions—like overwhelm, sorrow, or anxiety—weakens your energetic signal, which is the way you connect to and communicate with the universe. It is as if you are sending mixed messages; you desire something (like peace), but what you really want is control (which creates anxiety). This is because these types of behaviors (ones that have to do with what's outside of you) condition you to focus on reactivity.

When you apply the emotional-movement system called a Cleanse, which I share in this book, you create an internal environment and energy that can set into motion your heart's desire because you've created a space from which those things, people, and situations can grow. Then, when you go about your day, rather than rushing through tasks or avoiding feelings, you are more likely to enjoy the process and tune in to the little signs, synchronicities, and mystical moments. What makes these magical is the twinkle of reassurance and encouragement you will get when you see them. This is when you will know everything you desire is in the works.

Still, more often than not, some of the writing, podcasts, videos, and other teachings around manifesting fall short. First, many of them either assume you already know how to process (move) your emotions or ignore this essential step altogether. Second, they tend to make a loose connection between the way processed emotions energetically align you with the Spiritual Laws of the Universe *without showing you how to do it*. In other words, without awareness, even positive actions, like manifesting, can be a way to react and control rather than process and direct emotions.

Here is the thing: your emotions in flow, similar to an electric current, create a powerful energy. As this occurs, they become an incredible vibrational resource for generating love, happiness, prosperity, abundance, peace, and ease. As you enter—and, more importantly, *sustain*—these states of being through emotional processing, manifesting occurs naturally. The best part is that it arises from being your truest, most authentic self. In this book, I'll show you how manifesting through emotional processing not only relaxes and heals you but also expands your intentions and even your dreams. Your desire to have a high-paying career doing what you always loved evolves into being a compassionate leader; your desire to get married and have a child grows into an aspiration to be a patient, loving parent.

On the other hand, when emotions remain stagnant, they become something you must cope with and manage. This puts a lot of strain on you, causing you to leak precious energy, which of course comes with a whole slew of reactions, such as judgment, comparing yourself to others, and distractibility. When this occurs, you will still be manifesting—it just might not be the things you need or deserve but rather something coming from outside of you, such as what other people or society in general has told you that you need to be and achieve to feel peaceful and worthy. Don't take it personally; it happens to even the most well-intentioned creators; if this happens to you, it means you just forgot to charge your emotional batteries.

This is where some of the teachings of the Law of Attraction left me hanging. Very often, we're encouraged to focus on thoughts and images of things—a new home, a promotion, a big bank account—we desire. Yet with each of us having on average sixty thousand thoughts a day, this seems to miss the point (not to mention be next to impossible without inner movement). You see, the universe totally gets that you have a lot on your mind, but what it really pays attention to is your vibration. Here is the clincher: it is your vibration that builds your beliefs.

It is the difference between thinking you will never have enough money and believing you will never have enough money, thinking you will never have a healthy relationship and believing you will never have a healthy relationship, and thinking you don't deserve better and believing you're unworthy—Do you get the point? While some teachings about manifesting may encourage you to focus on changing your thoughts, I am going to let you in on a *real* secret: the movement of emotions will do that for you; the rays of light (which you will learn later) will help you sustain it.

Now, before you close this book saying, "This feeling thing is too much for me to work on right now," I suggest you try a simple version of my seven-step emotional-detox practice, which I call the "Cleanse." Take about five minutes to guide yourself through the following steps, and then assess how you feel.

PRACTICING A CLEANSE

Sit up tall, take a deep breath, and begin.

Clear Reactivity   With your shoulders back and down, draw your right ear toward your right shoulder, holding the stretch (while gazing to the right and down with your eyes) for four counts. Return your head to center, observe your breathing for three seconds, and then take your left ear toward your left shoulder. Again, your eyes will gaze over the shoulder and down for four seconds, and return your head back to center.

Look inward   Repeat this statement out loud: *How I feel in my body right now is . . .*
But don't answer the question! Just breathe.
Inhale as you inflate your abdomen.
Exhale as you pull your navel toward your spine.
Repeat this statement aloud: *And when I think about feeling, I feel . . .*
Again, only breathe here; don't answer the question.
Inhale . . . exhale . . . through your nose.

Emit   Inhale through your nose and make the "HUM" sound as you exhale, emphasizing the vowel sound, *hu-u-u-um*, as you pull your navel toward your spine and allow your tongue to move to the roof of your mouth. After the last HUM, pause and allow the inhale to rise inside you. Do this two or three times in a row.

Activate   See it! Visualize an image of movement, perhaps a babbling brook.

Nourish   Feel it! Allow the colors, smells, and sensations of what you visualize to come to life.

Surrender   Say: *I allow movement. I allow creativity. I allow energy. I allow freedom.*

Ease   Say: *I am movement. I am creativity. I am energy. I am free.*

How do you feel? Calm? Perhaps more centered and focused? This is the essential experience of how the emotional-detox process works. Now, here comes the cool part: you can use these same Cleanse steps to orient yourself with the universe—not in a superficial way, but in a meaningful way that can change every aspect of your life: your relationships, your experience of the world, and your sense of self.

Not only will you have an opportunity to process your emotions (which you now know can be calming to your system and useful on its own), as you'll see in this book, you will also gain a deeper understanding and appreciation for the Laws of the Universe and how they are designed to support you. This connection and interconnection can serve as resources for those times when you feel a little (or a lot) off track, need an energetic shift or some gentle reassurance, or have reached a crossroad in your life.

After all, life can be challenging. There is no denying it comes with its fair share of ups and downs, yet part of your manifesting journey is remembering that you are not powerless. You have choices, and one of them is to start digesting what you feel and turning those reactions into the energy that becomes action. I want you to know that everything you might desire—abundance, love, prosperity, balance, joy, good health, and freedom—already exists. It is not a matter of going out and finding it but of learning how to connect, embody, and receive it.

Please remember this book is not about getting rid of your emotions; it is about getting *to* them. Think of your emotions as buried treasures. As you unearth and understand them better, you will soon see how valuable they are. After guiding myself and thousands of others through emotional detoxes, here is what I learned: *There is only one emotion—love. Everything else is a reaction.*

SOME THINGS TO KNOW

Before you manifest, there are a few things you ought to know. Like, *What the heck is an emotional detox anyway?* and the language and terms we will use along the way. Understanding these now will help you assimilate the material more easily. Let's start with why you're here: manifesting.

Manifesting

To manifest means to bring something conceptual into the physical. For example, if you get a job offer, you may say you manifested it; if something happens that feels like it was meant to be, that was no accident. Manifesting is the process of transmuting formlessness—energy—into form: actions, events, habits, relationships, and even beliefs. Yet, often in the process, you can hit a little bump in the road. Perhaps you have a negative thought or go through a period when it appears as if things are pretty much staying the same or even growing stagnant. It is in these moments that manifesting may appear to take a turn for the worse, and before you know it, you start judging and believing you are attracting everything except what you desire.

Since energy is abundant and infinite, there is plenty for everyone and everything you desire. When it comes to the word *desire*, as you will see, what we are really focusing on is not stuff but on intuition.

The Cleanse

CLEANSE is an acronym for my seven-step mindful system that empowers you to give yourself an emotional detox and process your emotions:

1. **Clear Reactivity**   Disarm survival—fight, flight, freeze, fix—states. Center and calm yourself.
2. **Look Inward**   Identify your emotions (without getting into the stories and narratives).
3. **Emit**   Let your energy (vibration) do the work of transformation.
4. **Activate**   Notice, observe, and feel the rays of light through all your senses.
5. **Nourish**   Feel by allowing and receiving the vibrations the rays carry (for example, peace).
6. **Surrender**   Allow energy in action.
7. **Ease**   Be energy in motion.

Notice how your manifestations begin to materialize.

Think of Cleansing like repurposing a plastic bottle. Rather than throwing it into the garbage and letting it contribute to the pollution in the environment, you can choose to convert it into something useful and resourceful. As a result, everyone benefits from this decision. When we Cleanse, we repurpose our emotions so we can better manifest and access higher vibrations, guidance, and support.

Emotional Detox

An emotional detox is a mindset based on this truth: *all emotions are good as long as they are processed*. Its purpose is not to get rid of your emotions. After all, many can be incredibly nourishing and uplifting. Who wants to get rid of *happy* or *hopeful* or *serene*? Not me! Rather, the emotional detox is a way to release your *reactions* to emotions. Think of it in terms of food: fruits or vegetables that are sprayed with chemical fertilizers and pesticides contain a lot of stuff our bodies don't need. The same goes for emotions; only instead of pesticides, it is your reactions, like fear, doubt, guilt, or anxiety, that can create toxicity, preventing you from manifesting your best life. This toxicity most often shows up as reactions.

Reactions

Reactions are the ways you have learned (both directly and indirectly) to make the things that feel uncomfortable, comfortable; they are ways of suppressing or dodging emotions. **When we are in reactivity, it is a sign that energy is moving outside of us.** You can tell this is happening when you overfocus on your external world, for example, on a toxic boss or a dysfunctional relationship. For example, when something is weighing on your mind, you might stew in it—ruminate, rant, or endlessly replay the story. Some people react by trying to distract themselves from their feelings or thoughts instead of having them—processing them and moving onward. There are so many ways this can happen! Social media, keeping too busy, avoiding conversations, pretending everything is fine when it's not, mindless eating, losing our temper, and substance abuse are all ways we react instead of process our emotions. It is important to clear reactions as they can constrict and block your emotions. Anything that gets blocked impacts your manifesting potential.

Processing

Emotional processing is allowing yourself to experience a feeling without reliving or rerunning the narrative or story attached to it. After all, it is the stories (both true and imagined) that contribute to reactivity. While you may have learned in school or growing up what your emotions were and how to identify, label, and even talk about them, it is likely you were not taught how to *process* them. This is where the Cleanse comes in. **When we are processing, energy is moving on the inside. When it comes to manifesting, we are aiming for inner movement of energy.** You know you have movement on the inside when you have space between thoughts and you feel more open and connected to something greater. All it takes is about ninety seconds to process an emotion (even if it is from long ago). The seven steps provide a structure. Soon you will see how emotions in flow help you feel more grounded, calm, and relaxed. It is in these states of being that you can begin to align with the Spiritual Laws of the Universe.

Converting

You will also see the term "converting." To convert means to change or alter the energy into something new. Many people experience converting energy as an internal shift. In other words, you can actually feel yourself aligning with the laws. For example, you may find yourself detached from certain thoughts or worries (for example, via the Spiritual Law of Detachment).

When this occurs, know you are converting the energy into source energy. Source is the energy of creation. This is an internal experience and not based on any specific religion. The point is to go beyond any previous trauma to an internal state where your soul can remember pure love.

The Spiritual Laws of the Universe

Many of us are familiar with the Law of Attraction, but there are many more laws of the universe! These laws are the intrinsic and immutable truths that are shared by all religions and philosophies across history and are taught by spiritual teachers, poets, and even physicists and neuroscientists. The laws may have different names, but they hold humanity's common essence. In this book, I refer to the laws of:

o Divine Oneness
o Vibration
o Attraction
o Detachment
o Cause and Effect
o Correspondence
o Inspired Action
o Perpetual Transmuted Energy

- Compensation
- Relativity
- Polarity
- Giving and Receiving
- Rhythm

You may know them by different terms, like the "rules of karma" or "patterns of nature" or even the stages on the archetypal hero's journey, but no matter what name you give them, the truths are unchangeable. The terms I use in this book are drawn from the writings of Esther Hicks and Deepak Chopra, from *A Course in Miracles*, and others. I've also channeled and received insight about these laws as I've practiced the Cleanse and helped others Cleanse.

While the laws provide information about you as a spiritual (energetic) being, it is important to not think of them as separate from yourself. Just like the sun appears separate from you, remember you and the sun are both made of energy. Therefore, each time you reflect on how powerful, warm, and beautiful the sun is, you are simultaneously realizing how powerful and beautiful *you* are. I know this can sound hokey, but it is true. Unfortunately, society has blurred, obscured, and taken away some of the pure intelligence of who we are, yet within a few breaths, you can begin to reclaim it. As oxygen enters your lungs, your emotions will begin to move, and before you know it, you will be connecting to the creator that you are.

When you take the time to understand the laws, you are taking time to understand yourself. The cool part about working with them is they teach you about your soul's journey—how you are a spiritual being first and foremost—and therefore, some of the things you may have learned here on earth (messages intended to control or manage your emotions) might actually be oppressing, subverting, or obscuring your most innate powers. The good news is that your emotions can help you learn *and* unlearn ways of being, and as this occurs, you will naturally align with these laws of truth.

Trust that as you gain experience about how to work with these laws, you will develop a sense of grounding and clarity. As this occurs, your ability to manifest what your life needs will amplify. However, any confusion, misunderstanding, or disconnection from the laws can result in more inner conflict and confusion.

Let's face it, the Laws of the Universe can be fascinating yet intimidating at the same time—after all, they're vast and profound! Maybe you have dabbled in some of the teachings of the Law of Attraction, and I don't know about you, but it was always difficult for me to apply the teachings to daily life. Working with the Cleanse and the rays of light helps you change all of that as it deepens your ability to trust what you feel and your understanding that the laws don't judge or exclude—they guide you to open up and expand.

As you move through this book, I'd like you to keep in mind that you are a creator of energy and therefore:

What you resist persists.
What persists constricts.
What constricts conflicts.

Yet, sometimes you will also see "creator" referenced in another way.

Creator

In this book, I occasionally talk about the creator. Know that when I use this term, I am not referring to any specific religion; I am referencing the creator of *your* understanding. For some, it may be God, while for others, it may be spirit, divine power, or universal goodness. As you'll see, I mix it up quite a bit and have drawn information from all sorts of spiritual teachers, gurus, meditators, healers, psychics, and others. Some may contradict, but what you'll receive in this book is an inner-guidance system designed to help you reach the higher realms and an awakened state.

Awakened State

Finally, when I use the term "awakened state," I am referring to a place of awareness or consciousness. It's that area within where we can feel everything without needing to fix, change, adjust, or push it away. It is also a state of knowing. You don't always need evidence; instead, your intuitive senses provide the feedback you need to trust and be guided by what you feel. The rays of light, which I will define later, will help strengthen your energy even further. This allows you to feel safe and comforted so you can be patient with the manifesting process.

HOW TO USE THIS BOOK

Now that you are familiar with some of the basic terms and ideas, I'll share a few pointers for how to use this book.

Part 1 is the *why*. It covers everything you need to know about manifesting, including its benefits, an overview of how I work with the Laws of the Universe, and what gets in the way of your manifesting potential as well as what enhances it. I encourage you to read part 1 before beginning to Cleanse, otherwise you run the risk of getting caught up in the physical and reactive. In other words, you may not be processing emotions. When you neglect to do so, you'll grow frustrated. Don't force, but instead remember to *notice, observe, allow, and receive*. In other words, reframe making or wanting into moving energy and creating. At the end of each chapter in this section, I invite you to ignite an intention, in the sections called "Ripples," which will prepare you for part 2.

Part 2 is the *how*. Here I give pointers and best practices for how to do the Cleanse in all sorts of situations. Try to keep it light. Enjoy the process and don't take it too seriously. My rule of thumb is to do no more than two or three Cleanses per day. However, three Cleanses in one day is rare for me. As you'll see, it isn't about quantity but rather the quality of the time you spend.

Remember, this is not about fixing you; it is about you being *you* and getting yourself acclimated to these higher vibrations. Similar to the way your body has to adjust to higher altitudes, it also has to adjust to the reshaping of your energy. It takes time and dedication; having a solid structure to work from will benefit you greatly. I am incredibly grateful you are taking part in this journey. Trust that you have purpose, and that includes learning how to discover ways to support the movement of your inner energy.

PART ONE

Preparing
to Move
Energy

CHAPTER 1

The CLEANSE Method— Manifesting Version

If you are like me, you might have interpreted manifesting as the ability to make things happen, a way to draw something tangible to you, like a new car, soul mate, or your dream home. You might have watched movies and read books like *The Law of Attraction* or tuned into Oprah's *Super Soul Sunday* to gain a better understanding of how to apply these teachings to your own life. If so, I get it. I was right there with you.

I remember being so jazzed after watching *The Secret*. I grabbed my husband by the hand and said, "You've got to watch this with me. There is another way for us to go about how we do things around here." What I was *trying* to say was that we don't have to be so stressed-out about life; we can create happiness and security without all that mental and physical strain. This was typical for me; I was always looking to bring others on board to be a part of whatever I was focusing on. Yet, what I did not know was that this was just the beginning of discovering the world of manifesting and how all this attraction stuff really works.

Manifesting is the process of transmuting formlessness—opportunities, abundance, health, and more—*into form*. This is where understanding the Spiritual Laws of the Universe helps immensely. Working with them gives you the ability to reimagine how life could *feel* (as opposed to look). It seems the way we go about things now as a human species is to try to sort out or fix human suffering and environmental disasters by focusing on thoughts, problems, and solutions. What if we went about this in a whole new way, and applied feeling first? What if we all agreed that we are more than our physical bodies, and through higher-consciousness practices like the Cleanse, we can put into motion the things we all desire, like peace, joy, and freedom?

I found the answers to these questions in the wisdom of spiritual teachers and authors, like Marianne Williamson, who stated, "Our deepest fear is not that we are inadequate. Our deepest fear is that we are powerful beyond measure. It is our light, not our darkness that most frightens us." This helped me see the Cleanse as a structure for helping people connect, align, and create from their higher (loving, divine) selves rather than their lower (fearful, traumatized) history.

So, if you are wondering where exactly this information comes from, my best answer is that it came through feeling. Feeling is one of the highest states of creation—and it is from these states that anything is possible. It also came from *noticing, observing, allowing, and receiving* the guidance from higher-consciousness and divine-loving sources. Call them what you will (I often use the word "spirit"); just know true manifesting happens when we are connected (as opposed to disconnected) to these higher realms. If you are wondering why manifesting didn't work in the past for you, all I can say is that there could be a million reasons; there's one essential ingredient: the experience of the inner movement of energy, which can only happen from a feeling state.

Think of your emotions as a form or a shape. When they enter a state of movement, this shape expands to the point where it is no longer an identifiable form but rather a state of formlessness. It's similar to the way a cloud spreads across the sky. The energy of that cloud does not disappear, but the form does. As the clouds of unprocessed emotions dissipate, what you see, feel, and sense become crystal clear, like a blue sky.

When you react to your emotions, perhaps by judging or defending yourself, you are simultaneously resisting the process. You'll know because you'll start to question, worry, or get nervous about what you are creating. For example, you might muster up the courage to share your wants, needs, or desires with another person. In the moment, you might feel relieved to let them know how you really feel, but when you wake up the next day, you wonder if you said and did the right thing. This feeling of vulnerability and doubt comes from suppressing, ignoring, or minimizing what you feel. As you get to know yourself as a manifester, you will learn to trust and embrace this unfamiliar, new feeling. This is not a time to pile on more stuff into your life. This is a time to *notice, observe, allow, and receive* your intentions. Should those uncomfortable feelings arise, it is likely because energy is beginning to move inside you. Yet often people don't like the way energy feels when it is moving (at least in the beginning), so they resort back to old control systems.

So rather than *notice, observe, allow, and receive*, they return to what feels familiar, to what needs fixing and managing. This pattern gets the brain overly involved, which complicates things. This is because your brain (and body) contains emotional memories (some of them traumatic), many of which were never given the time and space to be processed. Without awareness, this can kick in old habits of suppression. Not only that, but when emotions are left unprocessed, reactivity (thinking, worrying) increases. This shows up in manifesting when people worry that what they are creating may cause more harm than good. *Strange but true.* Rest assured, this is not manifesting; this is perpetuating a cycle of reactivity.

Yet, when processing is not diminished or contaminated by the limitations of your mind, it becomes an internal resource full of nourishing insights, healing, ideas, connections, possibilities, and other good stuff. Here is the thing: your brain is capable of so much—from signaling that you are hungry to solving complex problems; it is not, however, so great at helping you move the energy of your emotions. *Why?* Because thinking is a reaction, while manifesting is energy in action. This is the state of consciousness I am referring to in this book.

In fact, scientists at Emory University recently published the first detailed view of the part of the brain that weighs and makes decisions: the ventral striatum. They described the three phases of effort-based decision making: the anticipation of initiating an effort, the actual execution of the effort, and the reward or outcome of the effort. This shows how your brain (mind) will always determine whether it is going to opt for something or not—like manifesting a positive family holiday dinner or working those extra hours—based on whether you were rewarded for it in the past. If family dinners tend to leave you more on edge than not, then your brain is going to judge, evaluate, and forecast whether you will show up for dinner or not. Here is the challenge: avoiding, judging, and anticipating negative experiences restrict the movement of energy.

SPIRITUAL CONFIDENCE

Have you ever heard yourself or someone else say: *I am going to manifest a . . . Let's manifest . . . I need to manifest . . . I am going to work on manifesting that?* I know I have, more times than I can count! However, statements such as these, when made without awareness, actually skew manifesting. It gives the impression these things don't already exist (when they do). The Spiritual Laws of the Universe teach us this. Getting to know these laws from a state of inner movement (rather than restricted movement) helps you to develop spiritual confidence—fortifying your sense of knowing, trusting, and believing. Something tells me you might already know you have these abilities; you could just benefit from some guidance on how to maximize your creative potential.

I once thought I could manifest money by creating an online course. While teaching is one of my favorite things to do, quite frankly, the course idea didn't really become a priority until I saw what other people were doing. I remember thinking *I can do that* and wondering why I wasn't. *They are clearly making a lot more money than I am. I'm behind the curve and need to catch up.* This is not spiritual confidence. How do I know? Because what I was trying to manifest was arising from a reaction of fear, comparison, and competition. That is the *opposite* of spiritual confidence! The reality is that there are numerous ways to accent your business or build another stream of income. Yet what makes one more successful than another is the quality of energy they are created from.

While setting goals or developing a marketing plan can help you get organized and provide a map for your next steps, these actions don't necessarily provide the energetic awareness you need to believe you can create something—that's what intentions do! When you have spiritual confidence, you are able to move at your own pace, say yes when something feels right, and say no when you have more than enough on your plate. You are also able to recognize what in your life has already manifested and how you wouldn't be thinking about or focusing on what you want to manifest next if it weren't already here. You are also able to notice when space is available in your life to create. For example, I know that when I have a light week with clients, that space was purposely placed into my life so I can focus on other projects or situations I am looking to manifest.

Spiritual confidence is the ability to trust the path, pace, and rhythm—not just occasionally or when something good happens, but also during incredibly challenging times. When you are spiritually confident, you are more apt to take time to notice when you are weighed down from carrying the heaviness of the world, to release it, and to clear (move) your energy. As you'll see, the Law of Divine Oneness reminds us that we have the ability to pick up both emotions and reactivity in others. Therefore, maintaining your emotional hygiene is important, and Cleansing does this for you.

Here are some additional ways reactivity shows up and what you can look forward to releasing as you Cleanse:

○ Needing to move on
○ Wanting to be in a better place
○ Trying to be liked (aka people-pleasing)
○ Comparing yourself to others
○ Feeling doubt or shame
○ Covering up or avoiding what you feel
○ Getting so caught up in the details that you lose your connection to the bigger picture
○ Judging yourself or others
○ Procrastinating

- Being pushy or demanding
- Walking on eggshells to cope with anxiety
- Making other people's experience more important than yours
- Being afraid that you are overfocusing on the negative

I call these reactions *control systems* or *management systems*. They are the ways you may consciously or unconsciously cope with uncomfortable feelings. While coping with something for a little while might be an efficient or even a good thing, without taking time to move your emotions, you lose precious energy and end up feeling constricted, overwhelmed, and even depressed. You may find yourself losing momentum as your sensory system dampens, and then bam, just like that it happens: suddenly, you are focusing on reactions rather than experiencing energy in action. Here are some more ways to understand the difference:

Outward Focus (Reaction)	Inward Focus (Movement, Action)
Thinking	Feeling
Doing, working	Being, creating
Focusing on results or outcome	Focusing on the process
Managing feeling	Allowing feeling
Wanting	Having
Feeling separate	Feeling connected

After Cleansing thousands of times with clients from all over the world, I have learned that once you process your emotions, the realizations that arise and the information you gather from them changes, and therefore so does what you end up focusing on. Let's say you are worried about your health and want to manifest a better physical condition, become more fit, and maybe lower your blood pressure. I could encourage you to imagine yourself as a fit person, tune in to the way you would feel, recite two or three affirmations a day, and visualize yourself eating healthily. Let's call this variation #1. For a while, you might feel better, yet without emotional processing, your enthusiasm (belief in yourself and the progression that would spark you to take action, like changing your diet or getting more exercise) may begin to fade. This is because (I'll say it one more time) your emotions also need to be processed, and when they do, it will not only help you feel better but also connect you to something higher, something greater than you.

As emotions enter a processed state, they take you inside the activity of manifesting. You will know this because your awareness shifts from what is happening outside of you to how you feel inside. You might hear yourself say things like, "I feel calmer, lighter, and a little more relaxed," and when you do, trust it is all in the works!

When you attempt to manifest something from your brain (mind), you see yourself as outside or separate from the process. This prevents you from experiencing these inner sensations. It won't be until you fully process your emotions that you will begin to realize that the energy of your emotions in motion *is* the vibrational state for manifesting.

Now try variation #2 (using the healthy body example) and take a look at how moving through the Cleanse effortlessly moves the energy without disregarding or avoiding the emotions.

Clear Reactivity Sit up nice and tall in a comfortable position. Move your right ear toward your right shoulder and hold that stretch for about four counts. Move your head back to center and observe your breath . . . inhale . . . exhale . . . Then draw your left ear toward your left shoulder. Hold on that side for another four seconds. Return your head to center. Observe your breath.

Look Inward *How I feel in my body right now is* . . . Inhale . . . exhale . . .
Now that I am taking care of myself, I feel . . . Inhale . . . exhale . . .
Living in a healthy body makes me feel . . . Inhale . . . exhale . . .

Emit HUM three to five times. Here you are releasing all your reactions, like wanting to fix or control your weight, inadequacy, or resentment.

Activate See it! Visualize a beautiful yellow ray of light streaming down (like the sun) through the crown of your head, throughout your entire physical body, moving outward into your aura (one inch to nine feet around you).

Nourish Feel it! Receive the confidence, inner strength, and resiliency that this yellow light carries by softening your shoulders and relaxing your face. Allow the vibrations to spill over into Mother Earth, like running water nourishing the world around you.

Surrender Say: *I allow confidence. I allow thriving. I allow flourishing. I allow freedom.*

Ease Say: *I am confident. I am thriving. I am flourishing. I am free.*

Take a moment to check in. How do you feel? Calmer, grounded, open, lighter? Notice the difference between variation #1 and variation #2. In the first, I encouraged you to recite affirmations and imagine yourself fit, healthy, and eating well to manifest better health. In variation #2, you went through the Cleanse, moving the energy (including any history of reactivity) along the way and cultivating energy in action. It is not that variation #1 is bad or wrong; it's just that the Cleanse maintains states of effortlessness—the ones the Spiritual Laws of the Universe teach—and that is where you'll connect with your spiritual confidence. Spiritual confidence happens the moment you recognize that what you see outside of you reflects the current energy inside of you and that you can shift what you see by nurturing your own inner energy, which brings us back to the Cleanse.

INCORPORATING THE RAYS OF LIGHT

Now that you are becoming familiar with how Cleansing works, let's look at how it can be adapted to bring you into harmony with the Spiritual Laws. Once again, you will begin with the C (Clear Reactivity) and follow the steps in order to the final E (Ease). Only this time, in the Activate and Nourish steps, you'll connect to something called the rays of light. While making this slight change might not seem like a big deal, I assure you it is. The rays of light are powerful beyond measure.

The rays of light are alive consciousness frequencies overseen by spiritual masters and archangels. Each color corresponds to a higher vibrational frequency. For example, the red ray carries vibrational frequencies of detachment, peace, and grounding in unconditional love. For years, I had been seeing these colors during *Savasana* (Rest Pose) at the end of a yoga practice.

I later explored the idea of connecting and seeing color through alternative healing modalities, such as Reiki, energy medicine, and quantum healing. While the courses gave me knowledge about energy and its connection to healing, it wasn't until I embraced the energy of my emotions via Cleansing that my connection to the rays deepened. In other words, I would no longer need to be in a yoga class or even see them in my mind's eye to sense the presence of the rays of light.

Yet, the real awakening arrived when a family member said a negative (at least I experienced it that way) comment to me. This person looked at me and said, "When was the last time you went to church?" By his tone, I knew he wasn't asking me a question; he was making a statement. Then it hit me one day when I was Cleansing, I thought to myself, *He thinks you have to go to church to cultivate a relationship with God.* While I believe churches do a lot of good for the community, I know God is inside of me. While I may never fully understand the complexity of the rays of light, the Laws of the Universe and the positive changes in myself and the people I work with provide me with all the reassurance I need.

Yet, I totally get if you are still curious to know more; therefore, I'll go into more detail about the rays of light in the next chapter, but for now, just notice how and where they are integrated into the manifesting version of the Cleanse.

Clear Reactivity   Open your neural pathways and redirect energy by connecting to the body and toning vagus nerve. The vagus nerve is the longest nerve in your body. It responds very well to mindful practices, such as breathing, stretching, and chanting. When the nerve is toned on a regular basis, it promotes a sense of calm and relaxation. It also helps free up any clogged or congested emotions. You will see each Cleanse offers a variety of ways to tone this nerve.

Look Inward   Turn your mind's eye inward to develop self-awareness and witness your emotions. *How I feel in my body right now is . . .*

The important part is to repeat the statement out loud (it can be in a whisper) and to allow your breath to answer the question as you inhale . . . and exhale . . . I love this question because it takes your outward focus and brings it inward. This is what the Spiritual Laws of the Universe encourage you to do.

Emit   Transform your energy by engaging with the present by humming.

Humming out loud not only tones your vagus nerve but also adds vibration. By adding vibration, you are opening a gateway, a channel, to higher realms. With practice, it is not unusual to see the rays of light pop in (through your mind's eye) naturally as you hum or after (when you are sitting in silence).

Activate   Here is where you imagine and focus your attention on a specific ray of light. See it! Know each ray carries certain vibrations, which will be identified in the Surrender and Ease steps.

Nourish   Here is where you will receive the energy of a ray of light. As you relax, you open your energy field so all living beings (including Mother Earth) can benefit. You will be blessed for this, I promise.

Surrender   As you surrender, let manifesting flow. *I allow . . .* Here you allow the qualities of that ray; you are invited to state these qualities out loud by saying, *I allow . . .*

Ease   Allow ease, and trust that what you desire is already here, at least on a vibrational level. *I am . . .* Embody this experience. As this occurs, you become a mirror, a reflection of these powerful vibrations for all to receive.

Think of Cleansing as spiritual attunement. You are adapting yourself to vibrations such as abundance, miracles, unconditional love, and more. Here is how it ties into manifesting: the car you wish you had vibrates with independence and freedom; the soul mate you desire attunes you with intimacy and love; the dream home you imagine contains the vibration of comfort, safety, and joy. As human beings, we tend to wait until we possess these things before we connect with the vibrations they contain, but the car, relationship, or house doesn't give you abundance; it just reflects the abundance already within you. Yet, if your focus is stuck outward, you may never really get this.

Very often it is not so much the stuff—the car, the relationship, the house—we want, but it is the vibration (feeling) we are craving. That's why people can have so much, yet it never seems to be enough. It is not that living luxuriously is a bad thing; it is when you have everything but feel nothing that you have to wonder: Are these things blocking or moving the energy inside of you? The only person who knows the answer to that question is you. Nevertheless, sometimes you do see things that unsettle you, for example an upsetting text or horrific news story, and this is why learning to ride the waves of energy is an essential skill to develop.

RIDING THE WAVE

Here is something I have learned about manifesters: they have huge hearts and big imaginations. While this can be one of their greatest strengths, when it comes to moving energy without self-care, you may find yourself resisting and, in some cases, self-sabotaging the process by getting stuck in negative thoughts and ending up imagining the worst- (instead of best-) case scenario. Part of developing your manifesting skills is learning to recognize when you may be losing your sense of balance and using the Cleanse practice to restore it.

Otherwise, all those good habits and intentions you wanted to instill fall by the wayside. I remember a client who said she was giving up social media. Then she met a guy in a bar, and he asked for her Snapchat name. Right away, she gave it to him, which of course caused her to break her intentions by checking Snap to see if he was reaching out. The thought of letting him know she was taking a break from social media never occurred to her; this is because she was still learning to recognize the signs of low (constricted) energy.

Without Cleansing, you are more likely to cycle into old patterns of reactivity, which often include lots of brain chatter—impulsive responses, self-talk, narratives, and even catastrophizing. Depending on the day, moon, weather, news cycle, what you ate for breakfast, or how snarky your teenage child was, you may find yourself reacting to those thoughts in a harmful way. Then . . . *bam!* Before you know it, you are stuck in the throes of depression or desperate to alleviate overwhelming anxiety.

Heck, we all react now and then, yet this is not the quality of energy you want to manifest from. Remember, reactions restrict your emotional energy. As a result, sadness remains sadness, anger remains anger, and this energy can take us far off balance. However, when an emotion is fully processed, such as sadness moving through fear to calm, it transforms into higher states of consciousness and awareness, which becomes the canvas you want to paint on. So, remember, processing (moving) emotional energy is a form of self-care.

Entering a state of manifesting can feel unfamiliar and may bring up some vulnerability. This is a good thing. This is the wave. The wave is the inner movement of energy that includes moments of being uncomfortable. Think about a time when you were about to do something new, like start at a new school, begin a new job, or go on a first date. There was a bit of nervousness, vulnerability, and excitement that went along with it. You were on the cusp of a new chapter, beginning, energy, or experience. Without self-care (and sometimes outside support), you can get overwhelmed with the process. No more! Each Cleanse provides the self-discipline you need. Notice I said "self-discipline," not "punishment." Self-discipline allows you to have balance, stability, trust, and faith, whereas punishment implies suffering.

What you are looking for is that sweet spot where you feel energized (which can come off as nervousness) yet calm and steady, and when you are there, you'll be moving energy. Before you know it, your intuition pops. When this happens, you get into your groove and go with (rather than against) the tide.

To support your ability to do so, I encourage you to get to know your bandwidth. In other words, know how far you can stretch yourself without reentering reactivity. How much can you take on and give without regressing to old patterns?

This example may help you sort that out: My client Anne wanted to move into a new home. It took quite a bit of Cleansing before she mustered up enough courage to start making phone calls to her bank and realtor. Up until then, she had been worried about how the transition might impact her finances and children. As she became familiar with the Laws of the Universe and Cleansing, her energy became stronger. Before she knew it, she was going through the process of house hunting swiftly and easily. Then she got nervous and wondered if she was doing the right thing. When I met with her, it became clear that moving the energy in this way was unfamiliar and new to her. She had grown accustomed to being in a state of limbo and doubt. This is when we had a conversation about bandwidth, which very much runs in line with the Law of Giving and Receiving. You see, Anne was using so much time and energy keeping all the balls in the air that she neglected to apply any of that energy to replenishing herself. I talk about this in depth in chapter 4, "Enhancing Energy," but for now, I want to be clear that there's a connection between self-care and Cleansing, and without self-care, you may find yourself resisting the wave instead of going with its flow. Should you find yourself in a state of resistance, recite this mantra out loud: *It is in the works!* Repeat it as often as you like.

Then trust that you can ride out uncomfortable thoughts by *noticing, observing, allowing, and receiving.* As you enter these states, the rays of light become so accessible. Those four ingredients keep you in flow so you don't get tangled up in reactivity. Instead, you allow the emotional energy to move through you. Otherwise, resistance may surface (such as self-doubt or fear), which puts you out of alignment with the Spiritual Laws. When this occurs, life feels hard, unfavorable, and difficult.

Remember: *Manifesting is energy in action.* As emotions move, higher perceptions (intuition) increase. In these higher states, you are able to notice (witness), observe, allow, and receive the process of transmuting formlessness—opportunities, abundance, health, peace, and freedom—into form. You may also create the opposite: take what is form (for example, a fearful thought), and transform it into formlessness. You are a creator of energy, and you can connect to other creators of energy both in physical and nonphysical realms.

Your energy in action amplifies your ability to receive higher guidance. This allows you to listen and lead from your heart, which helps you to:

○ Raise and hold your energetic vibration.
○ Follow and trust your own inner guidance.
○ Receive messages and reassurance from whatever guides you in life—spirit, signs, vibration.
○ Manifest from a space of effortlessness and ease.
○ Align with the Spiritual Laws of the Universe.

As you understand and have confidence in yourself as a person who manifests, you'll realize that moving your energy is essential to your spiritual development and growth. This will make it more likely that you will turn to the process of *noticing, observing, allowing, and receiving* as a source for bringing you into alignment.

The results will come. Have faith that the universe knows what you are capable of—probably better than you do! No longer will manifesting become just another thing you say out loud without having the energy to support your intentions. Instead, you will trust your path and travel it, because where there is trust, there is ease.

The most important thing is to keep your energy moving. Think of manifesting like a muscle that you exercise daily. One way to do that is to pay attention to ways you can cultivate inner movement naturally. To support you, at the end of the next several chapters, I have included a section called "Ripples." These are ways you can consciously choose to move energy. Making this choice has a positive ripple effect on the world.

RIPPLES: CURIOSITY

Take a moment now to reflect on a time you were curious about something. Perhaps you were noticing a beautiful flower, and you became curious if it had a scent. Or maybe you were curious about the temperature of a pond or lake, so you let yourself reach out and touch it. Notice how curiosity feels inside your body, the inner flutter you experience just by being open. Give yourself permission to be curious about the world around you. Ask yourself, What would it feel like if I . . . went for a walk, tried a certain food, turned off the noise (such as your phone notifications) when I ate my food, went to bed earlier, or decluttered my desk?

Today: Embrace moments of curiosity.

CHAPTER 2

How I Work with Manifesting and the Laws of the Universe

After a rough week at work, I was sitting in my favorite armchair gazing out the window, cup of coffee in hand, taking in the vibrations of the green ray of light. I just finished moving through the Cleanse steps to process my emotions. With the vibration of HUM streaming through my body, I was able to reorient myself to the intentions of *notice, observe, allow, and receive*. I had no clue what was going to happen next, whether things would improve for me. Yet my thoughts no longer matched what I was now feeling inside, which was calm, connected, and secure. I knew the best thing I could do was to let go of needing to know what was going to happen next and instead trust the spiritual guidance available to me (and to each of us) along the way.

Little did I know that *Energy in Action* would soon be picked up by Sounds True—a personal dream of mine. You see, I had a special connection to the publisher of this book. When I was a teenager, I looked forward to the arrival of the Sounds True catalog. My mother and I would snuggle on the couch under a blanket, oohing and ahhing as we thumbed through the pages. To us, the authors were like celebrities, and I would marvel at their new books and recordings. I never imagined (visualized) myself as an author; however, looking back I could *feel* it. The best way to describe that sensation is flutters of excitement—open, nervous, inspired, and grounded with a touch of vulnerability.

This is the energy of energy in action. I now recognize those sensations as signals from my inner spirit letting me know how to keep my energy in flow. Perhaps there are moments in your life where you felt an inner flutter. Pay attention. Notice how it arrived. Think of these moments as wellsprings for cultivating energy.

The difference is that today, I don't have to wait for something outside myself—even a favorite catalog—to arrive. This energy is accessible any time for each and every one of us. Align with the intentions to *notice, observe, allow, and receive* what is happening in your life, and you can experience it as well. Then, ask yourself: When have I felt this before? What was I drawn to in the past, and how did these experiences make me feel inside my body?

Even if you're not sure, something tells me your soul remembers. If it didn't, then why would you desire anything different? Here is the thing: you don't desire what you haven't already experienced on an energetic level. The Spiritual Laws of the Universe teach us this.

THE SPIRITUAL LAWS OF THE UNIVERSE

When I started investigating the Spiritual Laws, I felt like I was trespassing on someone else's property. The topic had already been written about by so many other authors I admired. Yet, each time I tried to talk myself out of moving in that direction, I found myself thinking about them. I have learned since then that this is one of the ways the laws work. If something circles back into your life, this means you are meant to pay attention to it.

The Spiritual Laws are so fascinating, yet they can be difficult to apply to daily life. Perhaps you can relate. This is because many of us attempt to interpret the laws from a state of nonfeeling. In other words, rather than listen (notice), take in the information (observe), and process it (allow and receive), we put too much effort into finding ways to control the process. If the Spiritual Laws of the Universe could talk, they would encourage you to let go of the wheel a little bit and enjoy the ride. Quit seeing the Spiritual Laws as a way out, and instead see them as a way *in*. When we use the laws as ways to get rid of our pain, fear, or frustration, they become an external solution for changing our life. A big shift happens when you approach the laws from a state of feeling. As a result, you have a relationship with the laws that includes rather than excludes (or judges) their wisdom. You also become really good at recognizing the intuitive moments that can inspire you to trust your path.

Before I trusted *my* path, I overfocused on the Law of Attraction, mistakenly believing I could use it to my advantage. Yet, what I learned is when you put all your attention onto one law, it is like reading only one chapter in a book; you never experience the entire story. Relying on a single law in any circumstance is problematic; that's why I've embraced and explored all thirteen laws to consider the fullness of life's patterns, reactions, complications, ethics, self-discovery, and growth.

The Laws of the Universe are a metaphysical system that was developed to help us understand energy and how it influences your thoughts, attitudes, and beliefs. Think of the laws as teachings, a curriculum if you will, about humans as energetic beings. Tania Kotsos, author of *Mind Your Reality* and *The Adventure of I*, explained this in saying, "The Universe exists in perfect harmony and order by virtue of these laws."

These laws have been recorded throughout history and studied by religious teachers, philosophers, and spiritual gurus of many faiths. As Tania put it, "Ancient, mystical, esoteric, and secret teachings dating back nearly five thousand years, from Ancient Egypt to Ancient Greece, all have this common thread." Popularized by the New Thought movement and spiritual teachers in the West, nowadays many of the interpretations of the Spiritual Laws have been developed and espoused by visionaries such as Esther Hicks, Deepak Chopra, Marianne Williamson, and Wayne Dyer, as well as a new generation of manifesters that includes Jennifer Pastiloff, Elizabeth Gilbert, and Sahara Rose.

Throughout this book, you will encounter my interpretation of the laws and how I use them to navigate my manifesting practices. All interpretations have been filtered and synthesized through the Cleanse process. The laws speak through vibration and feeling, and when you practice *noticing, observing, allowing, and receiving*, you start to get to know how the laws express themselves through vibration, eventually translating into thoughts, insights, and ideas that can be applied to daily life.

For nearly a year, Sunday evenings were a night of manifesting in my house. It was when I would connect with participants online from around the world to discuss the Spiritual Laws and to practice Cleansing with them. Participants were given an assignment and asked to notice and consider the way they interacted, lived, and interpreted how each law showed up over the course of the week. Some of them kept a journal of their reflections. Excited about what they were learning, often one or even a few of the participants would email me over the course of the week, sharing how they recognized the law at work and how they were able to respond harmoniously with it (rather than resist it). For example, when working with the Law of Polarity, one student said she realized she was expecting her ex to "wake up" and to realize he was making a mistake so things would go back to the way they were. She came to this conclusion after exploring the way the Law of Polarity teaches us about acceptance. In essence, she was the one "waking" and going in a new direction to gather the skills she needed to create the kind of relationship she desired.

Signs or intuitive *hits* are one of the primary ways I operate. I find the more you get in your head (analyze), the less likely you are to process your emotions. When you work from intuition, you are deriving information from that inner space I spoke about earlier. This is the space where emotional processing occurs. Reactivity causes us to miss those valuable signs and opportunities about ourselves and the world around us. One of those opportunities is to be able to recognize when an emotion needs to be moved. The best sign is when you have entered a state of reactivity (like worrying or distractibility). Not because there is something wrong with you, but rather so you can gain the energy (consciousness) to be able to see what is happening in your life right here and now.

If you feel you have missed some signs along the way, rest assured, there will always be another one that will soon follow. The Spiritual

Laws are always in motion, so you can bet they will find another way to get your attention because they are designed to work in accordance with you to help you develop and manifest your soul purpose. This is because, by virtue of being universal, the laws are based on a single truth: *you are much more than your physical body.*

Yet, when you are reacting to your emotions (rather than processing them), you are not living in truth; you are in illusion. This is when you become incongruent with the laws, which causes you to feel separate from them. A life of disconnectedness can make you feel alone, unsupported, anxious, and exhausted. As this occurs, you are likely to become attached to (rather than guided toward) achieving your dreams, goals, and desires. Getting to know the Spiritual Laws of the Universe will change all this, helping you align with one of our greatest attributes: vibration.

VIBRATION

Vibration is the energy of molecules and atoms in motion. Everything has a vibration. This includes your thoughts and feelings, the chair you are sitting in, the dollar bills in your wallet, as well as the emotions you may or may not be feeling. In the early 1900s, Albert Einstein wrote about how although energy cannot be destroyed, it can be transformed. When we apply this idea to emotions, we see that when constricted, they can make you feel stuck, heavy, guilty, or depressed. This is because as vibration decreases (in rate of movement), so does your level of consciousness and awareness, which means your experience is limited to what you can see, resulting in taking little to no account of what you don't see. You'll know this is happening when you don't see all the options, and this, of course, can leave you feeling stuck or trapped. But when you raise your vibration, you feel more open, balanced, and free to choose another experience. It is not that you change emotions; it is that the energy of the emotions increases in rate of frequency (movement), allowing you to have a new experience with what you have attracted into your life (perhaps a situation or a person). So essentially when you are experiencing an emotion (or having reaction as I see it), such as fear, you increase its rate of movement to create a new experience (but with the same energy), such as calm, love, or courage.

Let's apply this to everyday life. I once worked with a client who felt she had no friends. I took her through some of the Cleanses to help her align with the Law of Divine Oneness. Once we started to infuse the corresponding ray of light, I could immediately sense and feel a shift in her. The shift came not just from releasing and transforming the reactivity around her belief but also from the idea that other people would benefit from her processing of emotions.

There is something remarkable that happens when you realize you can contribute to a greater purpose. While bringing light onto the planet to assist the greater good of others may seem too good to be true, I ask, What do you have to lose? As Einstein said, "I like to experience the universe as one harmonious whole. Every cell has life. Matter, too, has life; it is energy solidified."

Here is the thing: when you suppress or repress what you feel through reactions, such as thinking, analyzing, or second-guessing, the vibration of those emotions decreases. You'll know this because you will feel separate, alone, or overwhelmed. This is because you are treating emotions as if *they* are separate, like something you have to get a handle on, manage, or control. Then suddenly your experiences reflect the energy of separation (no friends, no purpose, or whatever it is for you). As a result, your emotions don't get to move, expand, or transform in consciousness, awareness, or higher information. Instead, you might experience them as annoying symptoms or even physical ailments, such as insomnia or an ulcer. While this can be troubling, trust that your soul knows that you are a creator of energy; therefore, you are not powerless. Your soul remembers the importance of taking this energy—not to the origin of the wound or event, but rather back to the source itself.

Michael Miller, who is a writer for Six Seconds: The Emotional Intelligence Network, has said, "Emotions are absorbed in the body in about six seconds. If we are feeling something for longer than six seconds, it is because we are, at some level, choosing to recreate or refuel those feelings." Neuroanatomist and author Dr. Jill Bolte Taylor reports that it takes about ninety seconds to run our emotional circuitry—for an emotion to surge chemically through the blood stream and get flushed out. If the response (pain) of the emotion lasts longer, she says that it's because we are choosing to remain in a reactive state.

The point is that it is our reactions, not our emotions, that contribute to our mental and physical imbalances. This is because reactions take energy away *from* you, contributing to inflammation, which is restricted energy flow, while feeling and processing brings energy *to* you. Feeling (vibrating) is what creates the sensations of fullness and wholeness, whereas reacting and blocking vibrations create fear, panic, and despair. Are you wondering how the heck you are going to break that pattern? You can through Cleansing and the practice of *feeling*, which will naturally help you become more harmonious with the laws.

As you transform reactive patterns into a higher vibration, you open the way for new attractions, ones that reflect the new energy. As this occurs, old ways of handling and seeing things will change. This is because they are based on old patterns (from society, your upbringing, and even trauma) rather than the Spiritual Laws. The good news is that you always have a choice.

THE RAYS OF LIGHT

Eventually, I realized that the true purpose of the Cleanse and emotional detox was to channel and anchor remarkable energy (light) onto the planet. This realization came to me after a class I attended with psychologist Dr. Zoe Marae. However, it turned out to be more than a class. It was very informal, held on Sundays in the back of a hair salon on Cape Cod, where I live. It had randomly (but not really) come up in my Facebook feed. The fact that I was guided there was no accident.

Zoe has since passed away, yet her words often surface in my mind. She said, "Nothing comes to completion until we include

Mother Earth." She was talking about the cycles (patterns of reactivity) on earth. In other words, Mother Earth also needs healing, as she carries our pain, fear, sadness, and conflict. Mother Earth is one of our greatest teachers, illustrating the power of the movement of energy. Zoe didn't teach me about the rays of light—that would come later; and then one day during a Cleanse practice, something inspired me to integrate all three: Cleansing (emotional movement), the rays of light, and offering to Mother Earth.

The rays of light are the consciousness streams of spirit-matter that produce the universe. They provide channels for receiving energy from higher dimensions. You see, here on earth, we tend to oscillate in what is referred to as "third-dimensional frequencies." The third dimension contains two experiences, which can be challenging for us humans: duality and illusion. In the land of duality, there is light and dark (heavy) energy. For example, something like addiction might be considered a heavier energy. The heavier the energy, the more likely you will get caught up in illusion. Illusion is where ego exists. It gives the false impression that something is powerful when it is not. (I will share more about this in chapter 3 where I discuss the ways we block energy.)

The rays of light stream in from higher dimensions (fifth dimension and higher) where illusion and duality do not exist. Each time you open yourself to *noticing, observing, allowing, and receiving* these rays of light, you become a vessel for transporting the frequencies the rays carry (peace and unconditional love) to all beings, including Mother Earth!

The rays of light exist even when you are not focusing on them. Natalie Sian Glasson, author of *The Twelve Rays of Light: A Guide to the Rays of Light and the Spiritual Hierarchy*, describes the rays as "vast schools of spiritual learning and discovery." In her book, she states, "By connecting, understanding, and integrating with each Ray of Light, we can enroll ourselves in a special spiritual school that will accelerate us to achieve mastery, ascension, and new absolute aspect of the creator within us." So, think of it like this: if the rays of light are the spiritual schools (for universal wisdom), then the Spiritual Laws of the Universe are the curriculum, and the spiritual guides—including your higher self—are the teachers.

The rays of light are nothing new. They have been written about and studied since the sixteenth century. The concept has been referenced in several religions from both the East and the West. The New Age movement's metaphysical healing modalities, such as Reiki, popularized the amazing power of the rays of light. Therefore, much of what we know about the rays has been communicated and tested through healers, meditators, lightworkers, and spiritual leaders. You can see references to the rays of light threaded through Christian and Hindu scripture as well as Greek and Egyptian mythology.

I first heard about the rays of light while studying quantum healing. They were described as a gift, a resource directly from our creator. Quantum healing is a nontouch, restorative modality where the practitioner is trained to go into what is referred to as "the quantum field" to observe energy and use spiritual tools to correct imbalances in another person's energy field or aura. The quantum field is said to be the place where all possibilities reside. To do this, the practitioner has to be open to other states of consciousness, dimensions, and even universes. If you are skeptical or need to understand the science behind it, you may want to refer to the work of physicist and author Brian Greene, who discusses the possibilities of other universes in his book *The Hidden Reality*. In a talk recorded at the Museum of Science in Boston, Massachusetts, he referenced Albert Einstein, stating, "Nothing travels faster than the speed of light."

While writing this book, I studied diverse sources of information, and I found quite a few discrepancies in the research about the rays of light. After practicing the Cleanse around this, I was guided by my own higher self to let this go. The point is to help people manifest and attract the things, people, and situations that will guide them on their path, not to infringe upon their personal beliefs. I also found discrepancies in the numbering of the rays. For example, one source referred to the green ray as the fourth ray, while another said the pink ray was the fourth. My experience with the rays tells me you don't have to get hung up on numbers or order; simply be open to their meanings and be willing to receive their incredible light, trusting they come from a place of pure unconditional love and peace.

The cool part was that, as I introduced people to the rays, they got to know (and experience) them in *their* own ways. Their reports, higher insights, and manifestations helped me realize this was a resource that could make a big difference in so many people's lives. Cleansing opened the doorway (channel), acquainting me with the rays of light in a way that felt natural and easy to integrate into daily life. With that integration came questions, curiosities, and insights, the biggest one being: *Do you really need to focus on changing your thoughts (from negative to positive) in order to attract more of what you want or desire?* My answer is no—Cleansing with the rays does that for you.

You too can connect with these rays of light any time. All you have to do is bring yourself to a relaxed state; close your eyes; take a few slow, deep breaths; and allow their colors and sensations to come to you via your imagination. As you incorporate the rays with the Cleanse, you will get to know their sensations. For example, the pink ray (which carries vibrations of patience, divine love, and compassion) always feels soft to me, while the blue ray (which carries vibrations of faith, truth, power, and trust) has a thickness to it. There is no single way to experience the rays; just remember that their presence (similar to a sunrise or sunset) has a calming, loving, reliable nature.

As you sit in their radiance, you can allow yourself to download the vibrations they carry, which vary from color to color, like a computer file being downloaded. I like to describe the process as similar to layering on a second coat of paint. The first coat is processing your emotions, which can leave you feeling lighter and more centered, but when you add in the rays of light (the second coat), it's richer. You deepen and anchor your experience into sensations of love, peace, and compassion.

With that said, if you want to work on changing your negative thoughts to positive ones, by all means go for it. I will never try to talk you out of something that works for you. What I am emphasizing here is that it happens effortlessly through the Cleanse. If you are having a rough day and finding it hard to be present (even with the Cleanse), then adding the rays into the process really helps. They are like spiritual medicine.

Here is another way to see it. Think of the rays of light as functioning like a tuning fork. Essentially, a tuning fork allows us to hear a pitch and to adjust a musical instrument that has gone off key to match it, bringing it back into tone. It does this by releasing a wave pattern (electromagnetically), creating a vibration of disturbance in the patterns of energy (molecules and atoms), which allows us to tune the musical instrument. By sensing, feeling, and observing a ray of light, you are resetting yourself to resonate with the vibration it carries, like qualities of healing, truth, abundance, or miracles, and of course, intuition.

INTUITION

Intuition is more than a hunch; it is the part of you that knows beyond what you can see or make sense of. I believe we all have it. It is the part of you that says, "My gut is trying to tell me something." When you push away, ignore, or minimize what you feel, your intuition can become muffled or blocked. As a result, you may feel tired, confused, or frustrated, and you may not make the best decisions. This makes it hard to hear the signals the universe is sending, let alone interpret them.

The good news is the Cleanses will clear up those blockages so you can begin to translate those messages, signs, and synchronicities with more ease. Know that intuition goes beyond coincidence. It is the part of you that says, "I know this came from another place."

Signs and synchronicities are always occurring. Here's an example: Jim aspired to be an actor. He had a particular admiration for a star from one of his favorite movies. He discussed this with his mother one day, telling her how much he loved this actor, his style, and his choice of roles. When Jim flew to New York City to wrap up some things around his schooling, he looked out the window of his hotel, and walking down the sidewalk was the actor he'd been telling his mother about! He couldn't believe it. When he reported this in our session, we did a Cleanse on it, and the message he received from his processed emotions (after the HUM) was how seeing the actor made him feel equal. In other words, he no longer felt inferior. He trusted this as a sign that he had manifested his dreams. In other words, he was already a vibrational match to being an actor. This helped him continue with a sense of calmness and confidence that everything had already manifested, that it was happening. Now he just needed to take action, audition for parts, and enjoy the process.

I believe we all have many guides in spirit. While I have never been an especially religious person, I do experience the presence of Jesus as a strong, loving, and compassionate sensation. Of course, you don't have to have the same feeling or belief as I do. If the energy feels loving, calming, and grounding, remain open, *noticing, observing, allowing, and receiving.*

There are spiritual masters and guides who are eager to not only support your journey on earth but also to help transcend it for all beings. Think of them as your spiritual team, excited and eager to support you on your path.

So, if you are tired of all the noise and you no longer wish to participate in the conflict, injustice, or disease, I say turn down the noise (opinions, influences, social media) and tune in to your own higher knowing. Trust and follow your gut. If something feels heavy or off, Cleanse and receive higher guidance before interpreting (and acting on) what is happening. Clear your mind daily through these practices; sit in the rays to nourish your spirit. Allow the practices to tune your vibration to match your soul rather than what is on your mind. When you need a little pick-me-up, it can help to turn to the work of others, like Albert Einstein. Einstein stated, "The intuitive mind is a sacred gift and the rational mind is a faithful servant. We have created a society that honors the servant and has forgotten the gift."

Before moving to the next chapter, let me give you a glimpse of how you will be manifesting: Say you want a new home. Rather than tuning in to what you need to do (for example, earn money) to get that new home, instead focus on what you feel when you focus on the home. Notice your body. For example, when you think about purchasing a home, does it make you feel tight, clogged, or congested? Perhaps in your throat, heart area, or tummy? Just notice. If so, then it is essential you move the energy inside you. Your inside energy space is where creation happens. Once you move the energy on the inside, consider your energy to be in action. If you continue to focus on the money (or lack thereof), you will be in reaction. The point is to focus on the energy and then detach from the outcome; instead, let the energy of your emotions stimulate your intuitive guidance; then trust you will be guided. In other words, don't try to control the outcome. Make sense? It is all about moving energy and learning to trust that everything is in motion.

RIPPLES: CREATIVITY

Creativity provides an outlet for moving inner energy. You don't have to be talented or gifted in a certain area to be creative. Simply observe what you are drawn to and give it a try. For example, while writing this book, I was drawn to learning how to play the harmonium. Although I am not the best singer, the idea kept popping into my mind (intuition). Then an opportunity to take private lessons showed up in my inbox. Within a week, I had purchased a harmonium and signed up for twelve lessons. I knew the universe was attempting to assist me to move energy in a big way. So now I ask you, what are you drawn to? What source of creativity keeps circling back into your life? Perhaps you have an inner desire to draw, write, or cook. Ask yourself this: What if attracting that perfect job, soul mate, or home into your life required a certain movement of energy? In other words, rather than overfocusing on the "thing," instead follow your intuition. It will guide you to the source for cultivating the energy you need to draw these experiences into your life. Doesn't this way of manifesting feel so much better?

CHAPTER 3

What Gets in the Way
of Manifesting

I once asked a manifesting group I was running to draw two columns on a sheet of paper. I asked them to write down what they were intent on creating in the first column. I had them identify what they were putting their time, energy, and attention into in the second column. As you can imagine, I got all sorts of answers. For example, one person said they were creating the ability to finish tasks, yet what she had been putting her time into was thinking about ways to get a second income. Another person said they were creating a self-care routine, yet what they were focused on was how to recoup their business losses.

Are you seeing what I am seeing here?

Time and time again, what gets in the way of manifesting is confusion around what exactly you are creating. This typically happens when you make lists of wants and desires before you move your inner energy.

After I had the manifesting group process what was showing up for them, the common theme was "overwhelm." In other words, they were managing their feelings by listing what they wanted to create, which doesn't work. Once these feelings of overwhelm are transformed into states of calm and ease (via the Cleanse), your attention (*noticing, observing, allowing, and receiving*) is focused more naturally. Without these qualities, it can feel much like spinning your wheels. Sure, you want to move forward and get things accomplished, yet all the worrying, trying, listing, and efforting—all the management—expels a ton of energy, putting you more at risk for burnout and no closer to creation.

While we all get overextended from time to time, the thing to remember is that as you lose energy, you also diminish *noticing, observing, allowing, and receiving.* When this happens, you are no longer being guided to the source of energy you need to cocreate the things you desire. This is when obstacles to your manifesting potential may begin to appear. Some of the big ones are unprocessed emotions, addiction, judgment, and attachment, all of which withhold your light.

UNPROCESSED EMOTIONS

We are thinking beings—our brains are designed to think. These thoughts are ideal for making decisions (Do I want chocolate or vanilla ice cream?) and problem solving (figuring out directions on the highway). However, thoughts don't really help you process what you feel, and if anything, they prevent it.

What gets in the way of manifesting the magic in your life is when you only let yourself go so far and so deep. If you never allowed yourself to go into water higher than your knees, how would you ever learn how to swim?

Here are some ways you may suppress what you feel:

- Avoiding or withdrawing
- Minimizing or denying
- Distracting
- Diminishing or putting down
- Overanalyzing
- Complaining
- Blaming
- Turning to outside substances, like food or alcohol

Once you learn to work with the Spiritual Laws of the Universe in the way that I will show you, you won't be reinforcing any of these patterns anymore. There are plenty of Cleanses for you to work with, so trust that with repetition and commitment, you can retrain your brain to process (move) your emotions rather than react to them. First, since addiction is prevalent in so many people's lives,

I think it is important for you to understand (from an energetic standpoint) what may be happening.

ADDICTION

Here is what my guides told me about addiction. Addiction is the illusion of moving energy. Think about it: Why do we get addicted to something? There has to be some kind of payoff, at least in the short run. Let's take the example of social media. Here is what we know: each time you get a notification on your phone, you get a spike of dopamine (the neurotransmitter for pleasure) in your brain. Basically, you get rewarded for checking your phone.

Let's face it: rewards move energy. In other words, if I know working extra hours is going to increase my paycheck, I am more likely to hop on board. Yet, here is the thing: the sensation you get from moving energy doesn't last. Once you put that coin into the slot machine, get your reward, and jump up and down, the initial high dissipates, and then life doesn't feel so good. This is because the energy came from outside of you rather than inside. Do you get that?

In other words, the initial high is based on the illusion of moving energy. Here is one way to know you are functioning in illusion: you will always feel separate. Separate from the thing, situation, feeling, or person in front of you. The Spiritual Laws of the Universe (particularly the Law of Oneness) let you know that the thing you want so bad, the chase, the high, or the reward is not outside of you; it is you. In other words, when you perceive something as the source of comfort and pleasure (sex, food, money, drugs, alcohol), you are basically saying that those things (sensations) don't exist inside of me.

When you learn how to move your own inner energy (emotions, fear, pain), this will all begin to change, and don't be surprised if along the way you find some unconscious false beliefs. Addiction is very real and can be very serious. Know that you might need to seek professional help to further heal, but I hope this will help get you started on your journey.

FALSE BELIEFS

Beliefs form when you revisit a thought to the point where you accept it to be true, often without taking the time to feel what underlies it. No one knows this better than marketing experts. Each time a story, narrative, catchphrase, logo, or slogan is repeated, we are more likely to internalize it until we accept it as truth. Like the belief that Coke really does taste better than Pepsi. The same goes for manifesting. While tools such as reciting affirmations may be appealing because they tend to include positive words and phrases, if you are using them to override what you feel, they may just be a nicer version of emotional suppression or nonprocessing. Remember, feeling (rather than managing) is key to igniting the intentions of *noticing, observing, allowing, and receiving.*

False beliefs arise whenever you accept something as true without any real proof or evidence. They can be formed during traumatic periods of your life when you might have experienced relatively high levels of reactivity. This can happen when you don't understand what was going on or you felt your sense of well-being and safety were at risk—and this is not limited to physical safety but also includes emotional safety. Maybe you had some instability growing up. Perhaps the adults around you were going through a difficult time. This can be very traumatic to the development of a child, who counts on the adults around them for a sense of security.

False beliefs can also develop from society, news, social media, cultural messaging, and family dynamics. Again, if you see, hear, or are told anything enough times, you could begin to accept it as truth.

While you may not be able to control what you see on the news, what you can do is limit your own exposure, take breaks, and use other activities to put things in perspective. I recommend things like music, crafts, cooking, playing games, reading, and going for walks. Yet before we get into self-care, when it comes to manifesting, let me share one of the most common false beliefs: you *must* like all your attractions.

Let me give you an example. My husband is an avid cyclist. Biking clears his mind. One day he came home with a big gash on his leg. "What happened?" I asked. "A freakin' dog bit me," he said. "It came after me twice." After he cleaned himself up and calmed down, I asked, "How did that make you feel?" What popped out of his mouth was, "I don't know . . . like I had no control." Then after he thought about it a little while, he said, "I felt shocked." Here is the part you don't know: my husband was in a middle of a job change and was in a state of a lot of uncertainty. I knew that during the prior few weeks, he felt like his life was not in his control.

Did my husband attract a circumstance that reflected what he was feeling inside? Maybe, maybe not. When it comes to manifesting, here is the truth: you are not always going to like what you attract. The belief that you must like everything you attract is false, falser, and falsest!

Here is the good news: the Cleanse transforms those beliefs by allowing you to process what you feel. Saying that you feel like you have no control is not a feeling; it is a statement. It isn't until you process what you feel and align yourself with the Spiritual Laws—by focusing on your intentions while also focusing on the rays of light—that these situations, reactions, and patterns will transform into the quality of energy (vibration) necessary to draw in new attractions.

While getting bitten by a dog was very upsetting, it was also an opportunity for my husband to recognize some of the irrational beliefs and unprocessed emotions he may have been carrying, such as fear, guilt, or shame. Those irrational beliefs typically include words such as *everything, must, should, have to,* and *probably*. When you find yourself stuck in this language and glued to the story, there is a pretty good chance you have something coming up to process, and you can do that through a Cleanse. When you do, you will receive the energy, flow, and alignment you need to get clear, focused, and confident about what you are creating.

If my husband chose to Cleanse, rather than judge, analyze, or revisit what showed up that day, it would include feeling statements such as:

And when that dog came after me, it made me feel . . .
When I realized he bit me, it made me feel . . .

Once you Cleanse and process what is showing up in your life, you will see how events and circumstances can provide you (not block you) with the energy to bring the things you desire in a way in which you can recognize them.

Here is another example of how a false belief may get in the way. When Jenna was around her coworkers, she felt distrustful and out of place. As a result, she would have thoughts like, *Why don't they like me? Are they talking about me? Maybe I should quit and work somewhere else.* Managing her feelings of insecurity and sadness in this way took its toll on her. So, to help herself cope, she started to look into ways she could protect herself from other people's energy. She did things like visualize a golden light around her before walking into work. While visualizing this golden light seemed to provide Jenna with a calming sensation, the thought of needing to protect herself from her coworkers didn't really go away. One day, in a session, I asked Jenna, "Who are you really protecting yourself from?" Jenna discovered she was protecting herself from herself. In other words, it was her own fearful thinking that was causing her to feel the need to be "protected." Each time she focused on protecting, she pushed away her true desire, which was to have healthy, authentic relationships in her personal and professional life.

I totally get where Jenna was coming from. I was there too. I used to wrap my home, family, property, bed, and pretty much everything but the kitchen sink in white light before I went to sleep at night. Now that I follow the Spiritual Laws of the Universe, I still take part in spiritual practices (such as connecting to light), but I do it from a place of love, devotion, and commitment rather than fear.

Without understanding where your beliefs are coming from, it can be easy for false beliefs to feed your fears. Fear can be incredibly disruptive to the manifesting process, because wherever there is fear, there is judgment.

JUDGMENT

Kimberly, a student in my manifesting class, contacted me outside of class, forwarding an email to me that she just received from a family member. The email was full of reactivity and accused Kimberly of keeping the family from being close. I read the words carefully, tuning in to the feelings (energy) in my own body. Because I wasn't in a triggered state (like Kimberly was), I could see that this person was hurting. Had they taken the time to process what they felt before sending the email, the message might have changed from "How dare you!" to "I miss being connected to you."

While you might think getting such an email would interfere with Kimberly's ability to manifest, that is not the case. This was an opportunity to enhance her manifesting skills. You see, what you don't know about Kimberly is she had a history of shutting down her true feelings, remaining silent even though inside, all she wanted to do was cry, yell, and scream. Yet in this moment, Kimberly felt so judged and attacked by her family member that she was having trouble getting out of her own way, which is why she reached out to me. These kinds of rifts can happen in families. When Kimberly gave herself a chance to process the emotions around the rift and nourish herself in the rays of light, she was able to move from states of disconnection to connection.

The energy of judgment has an attacking, finger-pointing, putting-down kind of tone. It can feel cutting, condescending, and negative. When we are judged by someone else, the instinct may either be to defend, shut down, or run away. The challenge is that none of these responses matches the intentions of *noticing, observing, allowing, and receiving.*

Furthermore, judgment doesn't have to be about another person. Each time you judge or are hypercritical of yourself, it can also interfere with your potential and block you from putting your energy into action. Sometimes it is a good idea to hand the intensity of a situation over to your spiritual guides or the rays of light. Let them provide the love, healing, and support necessary not only for your situation but for all of those on the planet who are experiencing a similar situation. This allows you to transform the way human suffering most often appears—through states of attachment.

ATTACHMENT

According to the Buddha's Four Noble Truths, attachment is explained as desire, clinging, or grasping, all of which are at the root of suffering. Attachment comes from the part of us that so desperately wants to be seen, heard, and, ultimately, loved. Yet, our yearning for love can (without awareness) develop into unhealthy behaviors that make us feel paranoid, unworthy, and obsessed. Here is what I have learned: where there is judgment, there is attachment; where there is attachment, there is pain; and where there is pain, there is conflict.

You see, when we become attached to things, people, outcomes, situations, and even problems, we move out of alignment with the Spiritual Laws, particularly the Law of Vibration. This law reminds us that everything is in constant motion; nothing is ever static, even though it may appear that way. For now, just remember that attachments and emotional triggers go hand in hand.

EMOTIONAL TRIGGERS

A trigger is a state of reactivity. You know you're triggered when you feel emotionally charged. Something upsets you or gets you off on a tangent (like Kimberly). As a result, you have a sudden urge to either lash out, quit, or give up—this is reacting instead of creating. Some of us act on our triggers; others don't—it all depends on your levels of tolerance and stress and your state of mind and trauma history.

Think of a trigger as striking an old wound. You really believed you were healed, but then something in the present moment reminds you that those inner hurts still exist. This often happens because you never really allowed yourself to process the emotions around those situations in the first place. When emotional triggers are never given the time and space to heal, they feed attachments.

You can recognize an attachment by:

○ Negative, fearful thinking
○ Revisiting the old emotions, like frustration, anxiety, or anger
○ Being glued to one outcome or result
○ Getting stuck in the details

You can recognize a trigger by a sudden emotional charge that may arise as:

○ Tightness in the chest, face, or jaw
○ Ruminating thoughts, like obsession or ranting in your mind
○ Chronic overthinking
○ Flip-flopping or constantly changing your mind
○ Rushing to avoid feeling
○ Quick, impulsive, panicked, or urgent thoughts and behavior even though there is no imminent threat or clear problem

The real challenge with attachments and triggers is they separate us from the intentions of *noticing, observing, allowing, and receiving*. Instead, you may find yourself in the loophole of suffering, and I am sure you can see why this may not be the place you want to create from. The concept of attachments is a big subject with so many layers and viewpoints, and the Cleanses will help you dilute and transform those patterns. We will get to them soon. For now, I want to share one more thing that interferes with manifesting, and that is the way you may be withholding your light.

WITHHOLDING YOUR LIGHT

Your light is your true nature. It is the spiritual you—the part of you that is *aware of (notices)* your surroundings, that *observes* the moon, that *allows* yourself to be still to *receive* its glow. Your true nature includes curiosity, awe, wonder, connection, love, and more. You can tune in to it when you feel uplifted, and this is the state from which we move energy. These are the same states the "Ripples" practices (at the end of each chapter in part 1) are based on. Yet many of us lose connection to this aspect of our true selves. When this happens, we may find ourselves manifesting more of what we don't want. The rays of light help us return to our spiritual state.

Even children, who don't have all the responsibilities of adulthood, can withhold their light. They too can get caught up in doing, trying, pleasing, and competing with themselves and others. As you can imagine, this feeds attachment. You see, as long as you are withholding your light, nothing will ever quite feel good enough or complete.

Here are some signs you may be withholding your light:

○ You put your dreams, desires, and curiosities on the back burner.
○ You go along with things that don't really align with your values and beliefs.
○ You have a difficult time accepting compliments.
○ You feel guarded or protective of your energy.
○ You believe your time to blossom, grow, and expand comes later (such as after the kids grow up or once you move out of your house).
○ You are extremely careful about what you share with others.

Now that you are aware of what stifles your manifesting abilities, take a moment to ripple your energy, and then we can shift our attention to enhancing your manifesting skills!

RIPPLES: INSPIRATION

Inspiration is one of the most pleasant ways to move your energy. You can do this by listening to inspiring song lyrics, reading a good book, attending a conference, walking in nature, watching a sunrise or sunset, visiting an art gallery, listening to a sermon, or watching a heartfelt movie. Know when your inspiration is running low. Some signs include feeling frustrated, hopeless, or numb. No matter what your situation or circumstances are, you can pretty much bet there is someone out there who was in your shoes and has overcome it. The key is to ask questions and get to know those around you. Inspirational sources are often right under your nose.

CHAPTER 4

Enhancing Energy

I am on vacation and standing in my hotel room watching a video on my laptop as I march in place while slapping my hands to the opposite knee. My husband asks me what I'm up to. "You ought to try this," I say. "I am rewiring my brain because I am so anxious about how the kids are going to do sleeping here tonight."

"I am all set," he replies and sits down with the kids to read a book.

Vacations were not really "vacations" back then. While getting out of the cold Cape Cod winter and taking a break from daily life was nice, the reality was that we were still parents trying to figure out how to get our kids to go to bed in a new place. If I could speak to my younger self, I would suggest she stop moving just for a moment, sit down, and repeat out loud, "Everything is going to be okay."

While I am a big believer in energy techniques (some are incorporated in the first step of the Cleanse), looking back, I can see how much energy and attention I used to give to my anxiety. While I am sure moving my body temporarily relieved the symptoms, it wasn't until I started Cleansing that I was able to let frustrating, nervous, overwhelming, and difficult moments, such as these, run their course. In other words, I had emotions stirring in me.

The truth is, I was putting quite a bit of time, effort, and attention into trying to stop things (like sleep deprivation, disappointment, and normal ups and downs) from happening when instead I could have chosen to redirect my attention to what I wanted to create: things like love, connection, good health, and peace. I didn't have a doing problem; my challenge was on the receiving end, and getting to know the rays of light helped change all of this.

Here is the thing: sometimes we get so focused on what we want to prevent (or control) that we neglect to empower our manifesting skills—especially connection, forgiveness, signs and synchronicities, flow states, releasing time, and rest. Doing so allows us to complete old chapters of our lives and create new ones.

CONNECTION

Connection—to yourself, others, the rays of light, intentions, and the world around you—will be the heart of your manifesting development. You see, without connection, manifesting can be like handing the keys of your car over to someone who has never driven.

Sure, you might manage to draw in lots of money, attention, and even fame, yet without connection, things can get out of control. I have worked with clients who did well in the stock market, but when the money rolled in, their ego became inflated. This influenced the way they treated themselves and others. I have watched marriages fall apart when the "abundance" of money rolled in. What looks like abundance on the outside may actually be a sign of spiritual depletion.

At the end of your life, who you are won't be determined by how much money you had or the stuff you collected, but by how you engaged with others. It has nothing to do with your social media following or your latest promotion. As you move through the Cleanses, notice how you feel once you have completed a couple in a row. Reflect on the people you love and even the ones you may not be so fond of.

Connection is not about being perfect; it is about being real, raw, and vulnerable. It is about being open to giving *and* receiving. Each Cleanse will help you strengthen states of connection by allowing you to let your guard down and release reactions so you can move forward in a freer way. I always say, where there is connection, there is protection and an opportunity to begin again.

Remember, disconnection can happen, and we all have moments where we might say or do something that does not align with our intentions. Should this occur, simply move yourself through the

Cleanse and let the rays of light hold your energy in alignment with who you really are: a spiritual being. Here are some additional ways to increase connection:

○ Hugging
○ Smiling and laughing
○ Listening without interrupting
○ Sitting by moving water (a pond, ocean, or stream)
○ Noticing, observing, allowing, and receiving your breath
○ Giving praise and encouragement
○ Asking someone how they feel
○ Keeping your cell phone off the dinner table
○ Spending time in nature
○ Sitting in silence
○ Planning fun activities
○ Sharing a meal
○ Spontaneous engagement with others
○ Taking a class
○ Listening to music
○ Bringing plants into your home
○ Attending a worship service
○ Volunteering
○ Journaling or writing a letter
○ Sitting in (envisioning) a ray of light

As you nourish connection in your life, you allow yourself to be grounded in love. As a result, you may find yourself more open to other ways to enhance your skills, ones like forgiveness.

FORGIVENESS

When it comes to forgiveness, there are no hard-and-fast rules. Some people are resistant to the idea, while others may be more receptive. Some people can forgive instantly, while others need quite a bit of time. If you are open to the idea, it will eventually happen. I asked about forgiveness once when I was moving through a Cleanse, and spirit delivered me this message: *Forgiveness is not about letting go; it is about remembering. It is about remembering who you are and where you came from: love, pure unconditional love.*

Since you are reading this book and are interested in learning how to manifest, you should know that choosing to forgive will ease and enrich the process. It will help you remember yourself as an infinite being of light with unlimited potential. Right now, you may not know exactly what that means to you, and that is only because you are attempting to manifest solely from the physical level. I encourage you to focus on your inner movement. If you're not at a point where forgiveness of another person or event is achievable, that's okay. I once was there too. I always say that one of the best places to start is with yourself. Forgive yourself for all the guilt and pressure you put on yourself.

If there is a part of you digging in your heels, refusing to entertain the idea, let me ask you this: What will be required of you to remain in this nonforgiveness state? If you are not sure, may I point out a few things? It would mean you would have to:

○ Shut down your energy.
○ Bury what you feel.
○ Hang on to the past.
○ Revisit emotions of anger, resentment, and hatred.

Do you really want to do that? When left unprocessed, the emotions of anger, resentment, and hatred contribute greatly to attachments, which lead to suffering. The Spiritual Laws of the Universe are designed to keep your energy moving because they exist in the higher dimensions where unconditional love and acceptance are. So, in essence, choosing to hold a grudge may do more damage (to you, not the other person) than good. It can block your manifesting potential. Plus, there are so many people in the world who have had similar experiences who could benefit from you choosing to focus on becoming aligned with these Spiritual Laws instead of your hurts and suffering. Sure, your situation may have been difficult, heartbreaking, or even traumatic, and forgiveness might not fix it, but it can certainly ease it, moving you toward healing and a chance to change all of that and move energy. Once you make this shift, you will open yourself up to the signs and synchronicities around you.

SIGNS AND SYNCHRONICITIES

Signs and synchronicities are ways that our spirit, divinity, or the goodness of the universe speaks to us. This may feel like a message from a loved one who has passed, an epiphany, or a knowing. If you don't believe in any of those things, you may interpret them as universal feedback, ways to know that you are on the right path.

When your intentions of *noticing, observing, allowing, and receiving* are in tune, you can easily recognize signs. On the other hand, when your energy is constricted, heavy, dense, or shut down, you may miss them. Don't worry, they will circle back. The universe is designed to work that way. If you are unsure where they come from, remain open and trust they are from a loving source. Here are some examples of signs you might encounter:

○ Hearing a certain song that speaks to you at the moment you hear it
○ Coming across recurring words or phrases
○ Animals or birds that cross your path or enter your mind's eye when you meditate
○ Meaningful numbers, like license plates with the same three digits, repeating
○ Dreams that seem to contain messages
○ Coins, shells, or feathers appearing
○ Coincidences, like running into someone or randomly opening a book to a meaningful passage
○ A book showing up in your news feed that speaks to you

Once you start Cleansing with the rays of light, don't be surprised if signs and synchronicities show up more often. This is because your ability to visualize and imagine is growing stronger. This is when the magic begins and when we really feel we're in flow states.

FLOW STATES

A flow state is when you are in a rhythm, the "zone," or a place of deep inspiration or imagination. Things are coming to you freely and effortlessly. A flow state is where the magic happens. It is when you might ponder or reflect on something, and *poof!* It appears. For example, you think about a friend, and suddenly, they text you. You say to yourself, *That is weird. I was just thinking about them.* Is it a coincidence (sign or synchronicity) from above, or did you give that person's energy a little nudge to call you?

Flow states are states of creation. Whether you are actively creating something or not does not matter. You know you are in flow when you are more interested in the feeling than the outcome. Think of a flow state as similar to stretching your body. It feels good to stretch, right? When you stretch, tension gets released, and you are able to be more fluid in your own physical body. The same goes with your energy body: it feels good to let it expand energy and to open up your mind's eye. J. K. Rowling is a great example of this, when she imagined the characters in Harry Potter while daydreaming on a train.

Many professional athletes will often turn to their flow states to support their training. This allows them to go beyond the physical, expanding their energy in powerful ways using mindful techniques, such as meditation, breathing, or guided visualization, as tools for getting into their zone. Once in the zone, they visualize themselves scoring a goal or crossing the finish line. It is important to note here that practices such as visualization, meditation, and breathing put your energy in action. It is the inner movement of energy that helps the body and brain believe what they see as true (as if it were really happening).

You may experience a flow state when you are listening to music. Something about the music speaks to you in a certain way. As a result, you feel a connection to the movement of the energy the song produces. This can also happen during or at the end of a movie. This is because flow states open your heart. Your heart is a seat of creation. It generates powerful energy both on a physical level (as an organ) and on a nonphysical level as energy.

If you find creating a vision board opens your heart and helps you generate the movement of your inner energy, by all means go for it. The point is to get to know your flow state. Are you a daydreamer (like J. K. Rowling) or a visualizer (like an artist or athlete)? Just notice. Here is the difference between the two:

- *Daydreaming* or observing yourself in your mind's eye is another way to build your manifesting skills. Here, you watch the screen of your imagination, like a movie. You are not orchestrating what you see; you are allowing it all to happen on its own. In other words, you are drifting off, and it is likely what you see is playing out on its own without your direction. It is almost as if the flow state comes to you.

- *Visualizing* tends to be a more active process. You are picturing in your mind's eye how a situation or action could look and feel. You are actively engaging your senses and directing the process. For example, you may visualize yourself smelling a flower, dancing in the rain, or accomplishing something you've struggled with.

Each Cleanse gives you an opportunity to practice entering a flow state and can bring you to a place of releasing time.

RELEASING TIME

Right now, you may be used to measuring things like goals or outcomes in accordance with time. For example, you may think, *When I am finished with school, then I will get my dream job*, or *Once I'm in a relationship, I'll feel better about myself.* Here is the thing: when it comes to manifesting, timing is not guaranteed. The Spiritual Laws are timeless. The laws don't send you a manifestation because you turned thirty-eight and your biological clock is ticking. While you may want certain things on a specific schedule (and I totally get that—we all do), be sure to align with the intentions of *noticing, observing, allowing, and receiving* along the way so your goals don't shift into reactions. The Spiritual Laws encourage us to let go of attempting to control, and releasing time can help with this.

It is okay to desire a better job or to have a relationship; just be aware, notice, and observe whether the amount of pressure or the level of expectations you place on yourself makes you feel tight, worried, or constricted. This will likely get you stuck in thinking about and judging. The mantras you will be reciting during the Cleanse practices are "I" statements, as in "I allow" and "I am." "I am" statements are very powerful. They remind you that you are a spirit first.

So when you recite something like "I am worthy," know you are already worthy. As human beings, we don't become worthy; we shed what is getting in the way of us knowing our worth. As a spiritual being, you already have what you desire (peace, freedom, abundance, unconditional love). The point is, the thing (or experience) you wish to manifest is already inside of you. The Cleanses will help you uncover it.

REST

When you are in a state of rest, you are taking a moment to chill out, to relax your body. When you are in a state of relaxation, you are releasing your muscles and tension. For some people, this means kicking their feet up on a recliner, while others may find a bench or chair outside. It literally means taking a break. We all need breaks, and some of us need them more frequently than others. It is what you do during that break that matters.

If your relaxation time includes scrolling through social media, you are shortchanging yourself. There are many studies showing links between social media usage and depression. As you might have guessed, depression has very little movement of inner energy.

Be mindful of the amount of time you spend on electronic devices before bed as well. The point is to take care of your inner energy because your emotions play a big role in the way you generate energy. Research led by Antoine Adamantidis is "providing insights into how the brain helps to reinforce positive emotions and weaken strongly negative or traumatic emotions during REM sleep." As a creator, those positive emotions ignite your creative potential.

Here is the thing: if you are dragging yourself out of bed in the morning, pumping yourself with caffeine, keeping yourself busy with tasks, skipping meals, or eating on the go, there is a chance you could benefit from some extra TLC. Rest and getting a good night's sleep can help. You see, the less energy you have, the less stable and mentally and physically balanced you will feel. This is not the kind of inner energy you want to create from.

SPIRITUALITY

The spiritual laws are always there for us. Yet sometimes we might only turn to them when we "need," "want," or "desire" something. A way to enhance the movement of your energy is to find ways to incorporate the teachings within the laws into your daily living. For example, the law of polarity teaches us we wouldn't know light unless we knew dark. Yet it doesn't teach us to sit in the darkness. Just notice and observe so you can become better at allowing and receiving light. Ask yourself, *If this law could talk, what would it tell me?* For me the law of polarity reminds me the light is always in the present moment in the same place where noticing, observing, allowing, and receiving are.

It may also help you to know that spiritual practices can impact your brain in positive ways. "In a recent study of the brain done at Yale directed by Dr. Mark Potenza, *Neural Correlates of Spiritual Experiences*, scientists used functional Magnetic Resonance Imaging (fMRI) to examine exactly how spirituality activated or deactivated certain regions of the brain, changing how people perceive and interact with the world around them." What they found is that "spiritual experiences shift perception and can moderate the effects of stress on mental health. This study saw decreased activation in the parts of the brain responsible for stress and increased activity in the parts of the brain responsible for connection with others. A sense of union with someone or something outside of oneself and community engagement have been found to support a robust recovery from substance use disorders as well as other behavioral health issues."

Tips for Increasing Relaxation

Take slow deep breaths periodically throughout your day.

When your body is in fight-flight-freeze response, your inner movement of energy becomes clogged and congested. As a result, you may be more likely to manifest the things you don't want, such as negative thoughts, fear, and anxiety. Take a thirty- to sixty-second pause several times throughout the day to keep your energy in flow.

Empty your thoughts out onto paper.

If you have a lot going on in your mind, consider putting it all down on paper. This can provide a nice release and clear your mind so you are able to focus better.

Get fresh air.

Being outside—even if only for a few minutes to check your mailbox, walk to the corner, or sit in the car in the sun with the windows down—can help you become more present. Anything that brings you to the present moment cultivates inner movement.

Eat mindfully.

Simple things like eating in silence, sitting up tall when you eat, and chewing your food a little longer can help you digest your food better. The act of chewing more times per bite is a way to stimulate your vagus nerve (the longest nerve in your body), which helps you take your body out of the fight-flight-freeze response. Anything that calms your nervous system increases inner movement.

Here is what I know: when your inner movement of energy is strong, your thoughts decrease; this allows you to intentionally cultivate peace and freedom.

EMBRACING CHANGE

As you develop your manifesting skills, you will become more comfortable with change. In fact, don't be surprised if you find yourself headed in one direction when an opportunity comes your way, and you decide to shift. Sometimes people are a little hard on others and themselves for changing their mind. My feeling is that when you change your mind, it can be an indication that you remembered you had a choice in the first place.

As energy or vibration increases, it can feel like things are moving quickly. In other words, you won't sit in situations as long. For example, you may find yourself getting out of an unhealthy circumstance sooner or making a move that might normally have taken you a lot longer. Cleansing has a wonderful way of helping you take what you need—like lessons, inspiration, insight—and then helping you move on. I don't mean in an impulsive or unconscious way but in a way where you are able to feel confident, calm, and compassionate toward yourself and others.

You see, both inner and outer conflict happen when you dwell in reactivity. The dwelling (ruminating, worrying, rehashing) contaminates your inner space. This is because you are feeding it by giving energy to things that do not serve you or the planet. This causes you to separate from your soul consciousness.

The other thing about change is we expect it to be exhausting, disorienting, and painful. This is simply not true. Change can be a comfortable and amazing process if you take care of yourself along the way. The Cleanses help a ton. Again, remember to seek connection, forgive yourself and others, listen to the signs, stay in the flow, release time, and rest as you remember that according to the laws, things are *always* moving in a new direction, even if you don't see the evidence yet. Embrace your energy by practicing *noticing, observing, allowing, and receiving*. This allows you to get to know the Spiritual Laws of the Universe as the limitless spirit that you are.

RIPPLES: GROUNDING

If you have high energy, perhaps you are on the go a lot or take on more than you can handle sometimes. As a creator, it is important to ground your energy. In addition, if you are interested in spiritual tools and resources, like crystals, incense, and meditation, it is also important that you take some time to ground. Even spending too much time in the ethers (drifting or wandering) can cause your energy to become imbalanced.

Listen up, manifesters: grounding is important. This is how you create the ripple. It is important to channel the movement of energy to Mother Earth; remember, she is part of the equation of breaking patterns so we can all remember who we are at the source level: peace and freedom.

One simple way to ground is to stand up tall with your feet hip-width apart. (I recommend doing this outside with bare feet if possible.) Put your hands on your hips (fingers in front and thumbs pointing backward) and take three deep breaths (inhale through your nose and exhale through your mouth or nose). Imagine expanding the energy into your hands on inhale, and on the exhale, move the energy down toward your feet. Picture your legs as roots of a tree, grounding into Mother Earth.

This section covers the thirteen Spiritual Laws of the Universe. The description of each is a blend of what I found in my research as well as the information I have received from my inner voice, the universe, and channeled from the space of energy in action. The bullet points on how to connect and disconnect from the laws resulted from working with my clients. Over time, I was able to pinpoint themes. While each law is presented separately, they all work together. Like a family, they each have a unique personality but are at their best when recognized as a whole. The commonality between them all is *feeling*. When you allow yourself to feel your emotions (in the absence of reactivity), the system works beautifully. It is almost as if the Spiritual Laws of the Universe are a language that we can all understand no matter where we are from and what we are going through. Each one adds pertinent insight to the true secret to manifesting.

PART TWO

Cleansing
and the
Thirteen
Spiritual
Laws of the
Universe

CHAPTER 5

The Law of Divine Oneness

Tune in to this law . . .
When things feel complicated. For generational healing.
To connect to your divine self.

The best way I can describe the Law of Divine Oneness is as a state of grace. Grace happens the moment you realize that what you say to yourself is what you say to others and that what you do to others is what you do to yourself. In other words, when I put pressure on myself, I ultimately put pressure on others. If someone puts pressure on me, they are doing the same to themselves. The Law of Divine Oneness teaches us this. It shows that, at the core of it all, we are made of energy (atoms and molecules), and we are connected— we are one. Externally, we may look, sound, and behave differently, but at the core, we are all one. Of all the laws, I think this one can be one of the more challenging ones to grasp, yet once you really learn how to align with it, everything falls into place.

Before we dive into this first law, I want to be clear that oneness is not to be misinterpreted as absorption. People often think if we are one with everything, then we must be open to letting in everyone's energy. For example, if you find yourself feeling bad for someone else, this could be a sign that you are absorbing energy. Know this isn't your fault; some brains are simply wired to empathize (feel what others are feeling) more than others.

The challenge is, feeling bad is often a sign that you are reading their limited movement of inner energy. These states of limited inner movement are uncomfortable and can cause you to want to do something to make them feel better. Before you know it, you are so caught up in them that you forget who you are: a creator of energy. Empaths tend to go to the outside first by giving their energy to the person or situation to change the inner energy. While this may alleviate some of the pressure, it doesn't change patterns. The point is, the Law of Divine Oneness says that since we are one, you can alter what is happening outside of you by shifting the energy inside of you.

Rather than overfocus on what is happening to them, put your attention on noticing and observing what is going on with you. Then if it feels right, reach out and support others.

The brain will tell you that you are separate, yet the Law of Divine Oneness says we are very much connected, that we are one. The moment I stop forcing a separation from you and you stop forcing a separation from me, our energy effortlessly aligns with this law. When we try to control the actions or mindsets of ourselves (and others), we disconnect from this core truth, and we suffer. The way to align is not to force but to *feel*.

One of the most frequent ways I see people disconnect from the Law of Divine Oneness is by getting distracted. In other words, you may sense discord or anger and then attempt to manage it by avoiding or moving away from a situation. As you distract yourself, you become separate. I am not saying to stay in a situation that is not good for you. What I am saying is that the situation is not separate from you. Rather than distract, instead move the energy inside of you. There is a real opportunity here to make a difference, and your soul knows this. Align with the Law of Divine Oneness rather than push it away or pretend it doesn't exist.

You are disconnected from this law when . . .

- ○ You feel confined or restricted.
- ○ You are resisting your own growth and expansion.
- ○ You feel trapped and powerless (maybe you are numb or drawing a blank).
- ○ You are overly consumed with getting things done or obsessed with details.

- You are imagining what could happen, always wondering *what if . . .*
- You feel alone, separate, or disconnected (perhaps like an outsider).

You are connected to this law when . . .

- You are drawn to nature or to the outdoors.
- You embrace your choice to surrender.
- You have faith and trust in the process, and life feels lighter.
- You see things from a collective consciousness state (perhaps noticing larger group patterns).
- You feel a sense of hope.
- You are willing to let things (and people) go, trusting that if they were meant to be, they will return.
- You are handling yourself and the situation with grace.

CORRESPONDING RAY OF LIGHT: DIAMOND

The diamond ray is an incredible light source with pure, crystalline, and clear attributes. You may see the ray in your mind's eye or even feel its presence. Some people describe the diamond ray as translucent light with speckles of colors, similar to a prism. This ray is so powerful that it clears your spiritual DNA while igniting your soul purpose and promoting unity consciousness, which is the essence of oneness. Its strong energy helps you release old patterns, yet my favorite part about the ray and the reason I have chosen to link it with the Law of Divine Oneness is that it is here to assist us on the planet with the restructuring of systems. This includes political, environmental, and social systems. It does this by expanding our consciousness while providing energy to sustain balance so we can withstand and hold our light during times of immense change and challenge.

LAW OF DIVINE ONENESS: COMPANION CLEANSES

Cleansing for Joy

In this Cleanse, you will have a chance to explore the word "desire." Desire is typically a feeling of longing or wanting. Joy, on the other hand, is the experience of having. It is often said that you wouldn't desire what you don't already have. However, sometimes our desires can trigger old wounds and fears. For example, you may desire a new home. Yet subconsciously, the idea of taking out a loan may bring up all sorts of anxieties and fears. You may think, *What if I can't pay it off or something happens to my job?* You may also desire better health, and again, this may trigger thoughts such as, *What if this form of treatment, plan, or protocol does not work?* Joy is the answer, but first it is important to take time to Cleanse everything showing up around desire.

Clear Reactivity   Sit up in a comfortable position, with your chin parallel to the earth. Roll your shoulders back and down. Dip your right ear toward your right shoulder. As you do this, place your right hand on your left shoulder (holding it in place). Pause for four seconds, return your head back to center, release your arms, observe your breath for five seconds, and then repeat on the opposite side. Dip your left ear toward your left shoulder and place your left hand on your right shoulder. Pause for four seconds, return your head back to center, then release your arms.

Look Inward   *How I feel in my body right now is* . . . Inhale through your nose, inflating your abdomen, and exhale, deflating your abdomen.

How I feel in my spirit right now is . . . Inhale . . . exhale . . .

Tuning in to the diamond ray of light now, makes me feel . . . Inhale . . . exhale . . .

Emit   HUM three to five times, releasing all the reactivity, fear, and anxiety around your desires.

Activate   See it! Visualize the diamond ray (a gleaming transparent light) in your mind's eye.

Nourish   Feel it. Allow this light to touch the trillions of cells in your body, moving through you into Mother Earth and showering her with its beautiful light so anyone on the planet who also is reacting to their desires (who may feel ambivalent, worried, or fearful) may also receive the diamond ray of light. Allow it to disperse freely through you.

Surrender   Say: *I allow joy. I allow light. I allow energy. I allow freedom.*

Ease   Say: *I am joy. I am light. I am energy. I am open. I am free.*

Cleansing for Unity

Division is the feeling of being at odds. For example, you may feel divided from your family, the way they think, their political views, or their ways of seeing the world. Or perhaps you feel at odds with your workplace and the way things are handled or mishandled. While some division can bring opportunities for healing, growth, and change, without emotional processing it can also be a space where hurt feelings, resentments, and anger linger. The Law of Divine Oneness reminds us we are not really separate, nor are the words we choose to describe our situation. For example, unity and nonunity are one. Yet, what I have learned through Cleansing with others is that when people believe they are not united, it can cause mental and physical pain. In fact, clients have reported that when they tap in to the energy of nonunion, they can feel it physically in their body. One person actually said they felt a headache come on. Once you Cleanse it and gain an understanding of this law, these reactions slowly dissolve and are replaced by stronger movements of energy, ones you might experience as love and compassion.

Clear Reactivity   Rub your hands vigorously together for twenty seconds while breathing in and out through your nose. Hold one hand a few inches from your throat with your fingers closed. Breathe in and out through your nose while hovering your hand in this area. After twenty seconds or so, move to the next step.

Look Inward *How I feel in my body right now is* . . . Inhale . . . exhale . . .

When I focus on unity, I feel . . . Inhale . . . exhale . . .

Being in harmony makes me feel . . . Inhale . . . exhale . . .

Emit HUM a minimum of three times, releasing all separation.

Activate See it! Visualize an image of peace, unity, and harmony, perhaps individuals holding hands in a circle or a white dove (which, by the way, is the symbol of peace, prosperity, love, and luck). You may also imagine the diamond ray.

Nourish Feel it! Filter the diamond ray through you now. Practice your intentions of *noticing, observing, allowing, and receiving.* Let the diamond ray flow through you (like a channel of energy) down into Mother Earth, showering her with vibrations of harmony.

Surrender Say: *I allow peace. I allow unity. I allow rapport. I allow freedom.*

Ease Say: *I am peace. I am unity. I am harmony. I am free.*

Cleansing for Faith

To have faith means to believe in something wholeheartedly. When you have faith, you are less likely to waiver. Yet, so many people have been put off, deterred, and even harmed by conventional forms of faith. As a creator, it is important to have faith. Working with the Spiritual Laws is not about a specific religion or dogma. If you have a healthy relationship with your faith, this Cleanse will help it grow stronger. However, if you are unsure what you believe, that is okay too. The point is to give yourself permission to have the experience of the feeling (sensation) of faith, as it carries vibrations of confidence, conviction, and hope. Otherwise, you may find you have faith in some areas and not in others. For example, you may trust one person but not another. The Law of Divine Oneness reminds us it is not about trusting others or even ourselves; it is about trusting energy.

Clear Reactivity   Sit or stand up tall. With your arms behind your back, interlace your fingers so you can stretch the front of your chest and open your heart. Hold this stretch for about ten seconds as you breathe gently in and out through your nose.

Look Inward   *How I feel in my body right now is* . . . Inhale . . . exhale . . .

Sensing and noticing faith within myself now makes me feel . . . Inhale . . . exhale . . .

Now that I am open to trusting my own energy, I feel . . . Inhale . . . exhale . . .

Emit   HUM three to five times, releasing the heaviness a lack of faith (fear) carries.

Activate   See it! Imagine an image of faith. What would you see? A mountain or sunrise? Filter your image through the diamond ray. See it glisten.

Nourish   Feel it! Breathe into the rays of the diamond light while simultaneously allowing anyone who does not believe in themselves or who has lost their faith to take part in this experience. Allow this ray to generously flow through you into Mother Earth.

Surrender   Say: *I allow faith. I allow energy. I allow trust. I allow freedom.*

Ease   Say: *I am faith. I am energy. I am a creator. I am free.*

Cleansing for Peace

Rhonda has been a huge advocate for the environment since she was in high school, when she was president of the recycling club. Yet when she read in the newspaper years later that only 10 percent of what she was putting into the recycle bin at the local dump was actually getting recycled, her heart sank, and she felt deflated, confused, and angry. Apparently, if the plastic and glass was dirty, it would get thrown in with the other items. Through working with the laws and Cleansing, Rhonda gained a flash of insight: an image of her son (during the Activate step) in the future as an adult, unwrapping his food with a new recyclable (nonplastic material). While this was a wonderful image to see, it was the vibration (sensation) of feeling as if it already occurred that reduced her anxiety and brought her peace. When we see things like this in our mind's eye as our energy is in flow, it is an indication that something has already manifested in another realm. It just hasn't come into physical form yet. In other words, just because you can't see it doesn't mean it doesn't exist.

Clear Reactivity   Sit up tall in a comfortable seated position. Dip your right ear toward your right shoulder while dropping your gaze down toward the floor (as if you are looking over your right shoulder). Bring your head back to center and notice your inhale and exhale. Move to the other side: dip your left ear toward your left shoulder, eyes dropping down toward the floor, holding for about three seconds. Bring your head back to center.

Look Inward   *How I feel in my body right now is* . . . Inhale . . . exhale . . .

Having hope and inspiration makes me feel . . . Inhale . . . exhale . . .

When the earth is cherished and cared for, I feel . . . Inhale . . . exhale . . .

Emit   HUM three to five times, transforming old ways of living on earth.

Activate   See it! Here is where you might receive a message or see an image. Rhonda saw her son using new materials. You may see a clean ocean or pure, clean air. If nothing comes, imagine the diamond ray or another color.

Nourish   Feel it! Notice how you feel in your body as you connect to the diamond ray. Notice any inner movement. Relax your body. This allows Mother Earth to receive this beautiful light.

Surrender   Say: *I allow purity. I allow cleansing. I allow insight. I allow innovation.*

Ease   Say: *I am peace. I am pure. I am clean. I am free.*

MANIFESTING MESSAGE

When working with The Law of Divine Oneness, pay attention to the **ness**. The **ness** in this law points to the fact that emotions and intuition are an experience. It is a state of being. So if you were to take the example of wanting to get a new job, you don't *get* the new position, you *are* the new position. You don't *get* pregnant, you *are* pregnant. The **ness** is the experience of being one. You don't *find* happiness, you *are* happiness. You get the point? It is this state of oneness that allows you to embody the experience. You don't *see* the diamond ray of light, you *are* the diamond ray of light. It is an alive conscious frequency that flows through you. This law reminds us that it takes far more effort to be disconnected. It encourages you to remain in a state of connection, and this allows you to move your energy more freely.

Affirmation: I am one with the divine.

CHAPTER 6

The Law of Vibration

Tune in to this law when . . .
You feel uncertain or stuck. You feel alone.
You want to increase presence.

The Law of Vibration teaches that everything in the universe is in constant motion. Nothing rests. Therefore, nature does not intend for anything to be in a static state. You can apply this law in your life if you are experiencing physical tension or pain. Yogis and meditators have been working with this law for thousands of years. They know that in order to be present, energy needs to move. This is one of the reasons yoga came to be. It allowed individuals to move the energy in their physical bodies (via breath exercises and postures) so they could be present (notice, observe) in their energy body.

Yet this can be difficult if you are full of fear and tension. The tension gives you an illusion that you are in pain or discomfort, yet the Law of Vibration tells us energy is always in motion. It is not the pain that is the problem but rather the belief that it is not moving (or not changing). This leads to pain management behaviors. Rather than open yourself to what it looks like to be in alignment with this law, instead you can go off track (for example, spend hours surfing the web), looking for quick-fix answers. The Law of Vibration encourages you to turn to your own energy and let the movement of your emotions open so you can begin to listen (trust) to your intuition. I often wonder how much our physical manifestations are due to shutting down our intuitive abilities.

As you move along this manifesting journey, it is important to remember this: vibration is the energy of your emotion. If you are in pain, whether it be emotional or physical, you need more inner movement. If you exercise a lot, you may need to balance it with grounding exercises. In other words, align with your energy. The Law of Vibration reminds you to focus not on what you *want* but on what you *are*. In other words, if you want peace, cultivate your inner energy so you're able to recognize the peace that already exists. You will know you are doing so because your thoughts will become calmer, you'll become centered, and as a result, you will begin to attract what you vibrate.

You are disconnected from this law when . . .

○ You are thinking the same thoughts (perhaps ruminating).
○ You feel stuck (guilty, heavy, or hurt) in your life.
○ You are around a lot of clutter or disorganization.
○ You are easily triggered by others.
○ You are in chronic pain.

You are connected to this law when . . .

○ You notice the sensations in and around you.
○ You are engaged in practices that create inner movement (perhaps exercise or breathwork).
○ You are in a creative state (perhaps cooking, writing, or cleaning).
○ You respect, value, and hold space for your emotions.
○ You notice and respond to your inner energy (for example, you stand up and walk around when things feel tight).

CORRESPONDING RAY OF LIGHT: WHITE

The white ray of light carries the vibrations of harmony and discipline. Some people see it as a bright white (like a spotlight), while others see it with hints of gold mixed in. It is the ray of new beginnings and strength. Think of the white ray as a tool for spiritual alignment. When you feel fear or doubt about the future, the white ray can help anchor you in the here and now. I find the white ray links you to source energy like nobody's business, as if to say, "Remember where you come from, what matters, and your purpose."

THE LAW OF VIBRATION: COMPANION CLEANSES

Cleansing for Vibration

Have you ever been around someone who just can't stop talking? Perhaps they fill the room with useless chatter to the point where you feel like you want to run or hide. Maybe this person is actually someone you love, like you mother or best friend. If you are feeling drained after being around this person or situation, you may be wondering how to set some boundaries, not because you don't necessarily value them but more so to keep your own sanity.

Before you get too wrapped up in how to manage what you feel, consider if you have fallen out of alignment with this law. Here is the thing: people who talk a lot are often hungry for vibration (stimulation). Individuals who are irritated by the talking may feel like the talking is sucking up their energy (vibration). This means that each person is reflecting a reaction to low energy. This law reminds us that no one can steal your energy. Energy cannot be destroyed. Albert Einstein taught us this, but it can be transformed. You are not really "losing" energy perse; instead consider that it may be weak, clogged, or a bit low.

By all means, create the boundaries to shorten the visit, yet do it because it feels right. Beliefs and behaviors (reactions) reinforce the illusion that you are being drained. The Law of Vibration reminds you how invincible you are. Your soul has been through way more than tolerating a talking person. Don't forget how powerful you are.

Clear Reactivity　Stand up tall, with your arms by your sides, and spread your fingers wide, stretching the palms of your hands. Notice how this increases the length of your inhale. Then, on the exhale, close your fingers like a flower; inhale, open your hand, exhale, and close your fingers again. Repeat this a few times.

Look Inward   *How I feel in my body right now is* . . . Inhale . . . exhale . . .

Strengthening my relationship with energy makes me feel . . . Inhale . . . exhale . . .

And when I focus on energy moving, I feel . . . Inhale . . . exhale . . .

Emit   HUM three to five times as you release habits of controlling energy.

Activate   See it! Visualize an image of an open road or a plant with plenty of room to spread its roots. Imagine the white ray lighting up your path.

Nourish   Feel it! Allow the white ray to infuse you with high vibrational energy. Anyone who is feeling out of control or stuck in the illusion of low energy may also benefit from this ray as it is being made available to the planet through you now.

Surrender   Say: *I allow new beginnings. I allow energy. I allow expansion. I allow light.*

Ease   Say: *I am new beginnings. I am energy. I am expansive. I am light.*

Cleansing for Truth

When someone is sincere with you or you are honest with yourself, that truth has the ability to heal and transform all relationships. Yet so often for a variety of reasons, the truth is hidden. Sometimes hiding the truth is seen as a way to protect oneself (and others) from more hardship and pain. Other times, it is a part of one's own pathology or patterns. Nonetheless, when we veer from truth, it can influence vibration.

There is a saying: *you are as sick as your secrets.* Those of us who grew up in households where secrets were a way of life know how destructive they can be. You see, without truth, it can be very difficult to develop trust. This is where the ray of white light can help. It helps purify the past so you can begin to trust and have faith in yourself, others, and your pathway. It can also give you the courage to speak your mind and share your true feelings and not be ashamed to be who you are.

Clear Reactivity Take a moment to sit up tall in a comfortable seated position. Then give yourself a big hug. Go ahead. Cross your arms in front of your body and give yourself a nice big squeeze for a minimum of five to ten seconds. Release your arms, let your hands fall on your lap, breathe, and feel.

Look Inward *How I feel in my body right now is* . . . Inhale . . . exhale . . .

Opening myself up to truth makes me feel . . . Inhale . . . exhale . . .

Stepping into the clarity and closure truth can bring makes me feel . . . Inhale . . . exhale . . .

Emit HUM three to five times, clearing any reactions of fear or resistance.

Activate See it! Allow your higher self to pull up an image, perhaps an infinity sign.

Nourish Feel it! Tune in to the white ray of light. Allow it to penetrate your aura and the billions of cells in your body. Anyone who is also resisting truth on the planet may also benefit from this ray.

Surrender Say: *I allow truth. I allow light. I allow clarity. I allow peace.*

Ease Say: *I am truth. I am light. I am closure. I am free.*

Cleansing for Transformation

Even if you are wondering what transformation is, trust that you have already experienced it. Think about it: your spirit was transformed into a physical body. Your physical body has already been through so many developmental transformations. So if you are wondering how to transform yourself—perhaps you want to lose weight, get a new job, or fall in love—here is the thing I want you to know: your soul is drawn to these things because it is bringing up the memory of expansion. Your soul remembers how good it feels when energy is in action, and therefore, it will be drawn to the idea of being in love or finding a job that supports your passion.

Sometimes we are drawn to what appears to be the opposite, perhaps someone or an environment that makes us feel like crap. The Law of Vibration reassures you that it is all for you. The things you don't like in your situation are very often a reflection of patterns you need to clear within yourself so you can return to the memory of expansion. Make sense?

Your soul also knows there may be some things for you to clear along the way. You see, as a visitor here on Planet Earth, there are some things you might have picked up (for example, belief systems or genetic imbalances) along the way.

When you increase vibration in your mind, body, and energy field, it has a positive impact on your cells. Inside your cells is your DNA (genetic information). Therefore, the ways in which you choose to increase vibration can be transformational not only to you but also to your family line.

This is where the Law of Vibration and the white ray can help. You could choose to Cleanse those patterns (such as childhood experiences and beliefs). This allows you to align with the Law of Vibration so you can remember you are a soul, and therefore, most of what you are afraid of you probably have already overcome a billion times, yet because you are an infinite being, there is always more to learn.

Clear Reactivity   Sit up nice and tall in a comfortable seated position. Be sure your chin is parallel to the floor (neck is long). Use your fingers to rub behind your earlobes. If you are wearing too many earrings to take off, take the pads of your fingers and gently rub the skin under the lobes. Do this for about twenty seconds. You will likely notice a calming sensation.

Look Inward   *How I feel in my body right now is . . .* Inhale . . . exhale . . .

Now that I am connected to my soul potential, I feel . . . Inhale . . . exhale . . .

Transforming the energy in this way makes me feel . . . Inhale . . . exhale . . .

Emit HUM three to five times (or more).

Activate See it! Bring in the white ray, allowing it to dissolve and transform any negative beliefs. Note that the white ray can be quite bright, to the point where you would have to squint your eyes if you were looking at it directly.

Nourish Feel it! Notice how the white ray moves the energy; soften your body as this occurs.

Surrender Say: *I allow transformation. I allow purity. I allow presence. I allow peace.*

Ease Say: *I am transformation. I am purity. I am presence. I am free.*

Cleansing for Feeling

Feeling is vibration. That is it in a nutshell, folks. To feel means to vibrate internally. As a human being, you can tune in to the vibration via your senses: your sense of smell, touch, and taste, and your sense of energy. Intuition helps you understand yourself as a vibrational (feeling) being. The Spiritual Law of Vibration reminds us of this more than anything. Yet, so many of us were taught what to feel and what not to feel.

I remember asking a teenage boy how he felt about something. Immediately, he went to his thinking brain. He looked upward with his eyes and started to search for the answer. Then I jokingly said to him, "The feelings aren't in your head." He still had no clue how to respond to the question, so then I asked him to visualize the color green. I noticed his eyes became soft and looked outward (rather than upward). "Do you see it?" I asked. He responded yes. Then I asked again, "Tell me now how you feel." This time he was able to describe feeling calm and present.

To put it in manifesting terms, if you want to increase something, like calm and peace, yet you find yourself managing your emotions (by turning to your thoughts), then it would make sense that you are frustrated with your progress. People do this all the time. For example, they may keep an employee on board or hang onto a toxic relationship because they think the situation will improve. Yet if the person is not performing or measuring up to your needs, your energy can get impacted. Listen, I get it. No one wants to look like "the bad guy." The good news is that invoking the white ray into your situation not only helps you clear what is blocking you so you can create the life you desire, but it also helps the person you may be protecting from feeling hurt or disappointment. It is not your job to figure out what is next for someone or what job fits their style. It is your job to expand and move your own energy.

Clear Reactivity   Take a moment to interlace your hands and draw them up over head so you can get a big stretch. Hold this stretch for ten seconds and then release. Place your hands in your lap while sitting up tall, and inhale slowly (inflate your abdominals) for the count of three and exhale (deflate your abdominals, moving your navel toward your spine) for the count of three.

Look Inward   *How I feel in my body right now is* . . . Inhale . . . exhale . . .

Now that I am no longer holding back my emotions, I feel . . . Inhale . . exhale . . .

Drawing upon the white ray of light to bring purity and peace to the situation now makes me feel . . . Inhale . . . exhale . . .

Emit   HUM three to five times or more.

Activate   See it! Imagine a beautiful white light in your mind's eye.

Nourish   Feel it! Notice how sitting in white light makes you feel. Do you feel lighter? Let these sensations spread to the world.

Surrender Say: *I allow purity. I allow feeling. I allow opening. I allow ease.*

Ease Say: *I am purity. I am new beginnings. I am vibration. I am feeling. I am free.*

MANIFESTING MESSAGE

You will know you have processed a feeling because you will no longer be interested in repeating a story or narrative. If you were to put your attention on the story, you would notice it has less of a charge. In other words, it no longer distracts you or takes you off your path. The white ray is ideal as it purifies what is not serving you while holding you in the here and now, the place where no negative stories or beliefs exist.

Affirmation: I am energy in motion.

CHAPTER 7

The Law of Attraction

Tune in to this law to . . .
Strengthen your magnetic energy. Increase confidence.
Release restrictions.

Of all the Spiritual Laws, this one seems to have gotten the most attention. At a very basic level, the Law of Attraction teaches that what you focus on expands. In other words, whatever you give your time, attention, and energy to will inevitably expand, increase, and grow. Therefore, if you dwell on what you don't have or how exhausted you are, you will draw more experiences of feeling depletion.

Many people who teach the Law of Attraction suggest focusing on visualizations as a tool for amplifying the ability to draw in more of what you want (such as to find a soul mate) and desire (to be happy). Here is the challenge: if you are reacting to your feelings or others, you could be focusing on blocked energy.

As a result, you may draw in blocked energy. This can show up many ways. In my experience, some people actually feel the blocked (fearful) energy of others. I once had a client who went to the dentist feeling perfectly fine. When she left, she felt a heaviness inside her to the point where she ended up not being able to go back to work. Once we Cleansed it, she realized she was so tuned in to the dental assistant's energy that she took it upon herself. If you were to look at this from the Law of Attraction viewpoint, she focused on the blocked heavy energy she was picking up on, and by focusing on it, she expanded it.

Here is how I like to work with the Law of Attraction. Rather than focus on what I want (let's say to increase my customers or clients), instead I put more attention on the things, situations, and experiences that open up my field of energy. For example, if someone says something kind or I eat a really good meal, I make sure to take a moment to really take in how good it feels to move energy in this way. Food becomes a resource for having a relationship with my inner energy rather than a control system. I know that if the energy is expanding inside of me, I can be, do, and have anything I want, and by the way, so can you. Think about it, there are people with no arms and legs out there in the world who teach themselves how to swim. If they can do it, so can you.

The good news is that each time you focus on a ray of light you are in essence concentrating on the vibrations it carries. In this case, the yellow ray of light carries resilience, hope, and nonjudgment. When you focus on a ray, you are focusing on expanded energy. See how simple that can be.

Before you know it, you will realize how easily things are flowing to you, almost as if you are being guided and supported every step of the way—which you are! You will take action, but it will come from a place of being in alignment with higher energy. Sure, now and then you may get a little off track here or there; we all do. Cleanse and reconnect to the intentions of *noticing, observing, allowing, and receiving.* This allows you to work optimally with this law.

You are disconnected from this law when . . .

○ You do things in excess (perhaps eating, drinking, or using social media).
○ You feel like you are on the edge of a crisis or that something bad might happen.
○ You are overly consumed with the outside (how you appear to others).
○ You overpower your emotions with your mind (thoughts).
○ You rescue others from their feelings (and as a way to manage yours).

- You judge, criticize, or label your attractions (and your emotions).
- You take things too seriously.
- You feel like you want to run or push others away.
- You are trying to do (attract) too many things at one time.

You are connected to this law when . . .

- You are open to being and feeling vulnerable.
- You are able to soften, relax, and be present.
- You notice your discomfort without judgment or the need to make it stop.
- You are curious and open to all your attractions.
- You follow what feels right.
- You notice coincidences, signs, and signals from the universe.
- You are more interested in being yourself.
- You are able to be playful and allow fun and laughter along the way.
- You choose to focus on connection.

CORRESPONDING RAY OF LIGHT: YELLOW

I like to describe the yellow ray as a builder. It builds you up during or after times of stress, overwhelm, or confusion. Similar to the way calcium keeps your bones strong, the yellow ray of light gives you inner strength, confidence, and wisdom. As confidence comes, so do focus and clarity. This is because the yellow ray vibrates unconditional love and nonjudgment and therefore has a way of refreshing your ideas and thoughts from fearful and overwhelming to beautiful. So, if realizing your situation could benefit from discernment, stamina, resiliency, courage, or energy, the yellow ray will provide you with just that and more. Not to mention, this ray is known for its manifesting potential.

THE LAW OF ATTRACTION: COMPANION CLEANSES

Cleansing for Compassion

Miranda thought she was doing the right thing when she texted her boyfriend to let him know she felt sad. He had let her know the importance of having an open and honest relationship. Yet, when he returned her texts with a slew of reactions, accusing her of trying to ruin his good time with his friends, Miranda found herself feeling upset and defensive.

What started out as wanting to be intimate and transparent turned into a nasty argument. Surely you can relate to those times when you make a move only to regret it later. Here is the thing: when it comes to the Law of Attraction, having compassion for yourself is key. The reason why some attractions (situations and events) in our lives can be so intense and at times darn-right uncomfortable is because they are part of a collective pattern. It is important to remember that each time you Cleanse, you are bringing incredible rays of light to the planet. It can be so tempting to focus on who said what, how, and when. Remember, as you bring the light in, dark, heavy emotions will lift. While it might not look like you are manifesting (attracting) what you want in the moment, it is important that you stay calm and centered and allow yourself to respond to yourself with love and compassion. It is all in the works; trust it, and Cleanse.

Clear Reactivity   Sit up tall in a comfortable position. Make loose fists with your hands. Similar to the way you would quietly knock on someone's door, with your fists, gently tap your chest (above the heart), moving the energy between your shoulders, for about twenty seconds. Place your hands on your lap and relax your facial muscles.

Look Inward   *How I feel in my body right now is . . .* Inhale . . . exhale . . .

Building myself up in this way makes me feel . . . Inhale . . . exhale . . .

Recognizing and transforming this pattern now makes me feel . . . Inhale . . . exhale . . .

Emit   HUM three to five times, as you release and transform reactions, such as managing and defensiveness, into inner strength.

Activate   See it! Visualize an image of compassion, perhaps an image of holding hands or patting someone gently on the back. Imagine the yellow ray.

Nourish   Feel it! Filter the sensations of the yellow ray into your cells; allow it to nourish you with inner strength, resiliency, and confidence. May anyone who is managing emotions of others on the planet also receive the opportunity to receive the vibrations of this ray.

Surrender   Say: *I allow compassion. I allow love. I allow grounding. I allow growth.*

Ease   Say: *I am growth. I am compassion. I am inner strength. I am free,*

Cleansing for Revelation

Do you sometimes keep what you really think and feel hidden from the surface? Are there feelings, memories, or experiences inside of you that you have covered up or kept to yourself? What is preventing you from sharing your experiences and stories with others? These are the kinds of patterns that can block your energy and, without awareness, stifle your ability to create.

You see, there are special powers inside of you. Among these is the ability to pick up on, transform, and transmute energy. Manifesting is about revealing. Think about it: you can't hide and bring something into the physical at the same time. This is because keeping your guard up means there is a part of you that resists what you are feeling. You can't create what you don't feel. This Cleanse will help you let your guard down, release, relax, and renew so you can begin to accept and embrace yourself fully as a manifester. Let's do this!

Clear Reactivity   Sit up tall in a comfortable position, and place your hands on top of your heart center, one on top of the other. Inhale through your nose (inflating your abdomen) and on the exhale, release your jaw, exhaling out of your mouth. You will be inhaling with your mouth closed and exhaling with it open. Breathe mindfully and slowly, three or four times. Pause before you move to the next step.

Look Inward *How I feel in my body right now is* . . . Inhale . . . exhale . . .

And when I hide my truth, I feel . . . Inhale . . . exhale . . .

Now that I am opening and willing to reveal my true self, I feel . . . Inhale . . . exhale . . .

Emit HUM three to five times as you release and transform hiding to revealing.

Activate See it! Visualize an image of revelation, perhaps a profound moment where you would be able to believe something is true, an image of rebirth or renewal, or the color yellow.

Nourish Feel it! Notice what the yellow ray feels like: warm, comforting, safe. Just notice.

Surrender Say: *I allow sparkle. I allow life. I allow revealing. I allow faith.*

Ease Say: *I am life. I am open. I am revelation. I am free.*

Cleansing for a Shift

"Take me through the process," I said. "Tell me what happens before you binge." Step by step, Natalia gave me a detailed description of the way she handled her food cravings. This included the thoughts that went through her head, the way she snuck out of the house when she believed no one would know, the order she would place at the fast food drive-through, as well as the immense guilt and shame she would be left to manage soon after. She also described the habit of sleeping in after an exhausting night of torturing herself mentally and stewing in the toxicity. There was a lot that needed to shift.

When it comes to manifesting, I find shifting happens more naturally than changing. When you focus on change, this means there has to be a part of you that doesn't like what you see. On the other hand, to shift means to become aware or to expand the way you think or do things. Think of a shift as an opening, an inner space inside of you where you can allow the light to come in. When you think shift, think small. It could be as simple as changing your seat so you can see the world from a different angle. Keep things light and tangible and let the Spiritual Laws of the Universe and the Cleanse do the rest.

Clear Reactivity   Sit or stand up tall. Open your mouth wide, and make an AHH sound, similar to the way you might blow air out of your mouth to fog a mirror. Inhale and repeat this three to four times. Your navel will move toward your spine on the exhale.

Look Inward   *How I feel in my body right now is* . . . Inhale . . . exhale . . .

Opening myself to an internal shift now makes me feel . . . Inhale . . . exhale . . .

And when I allow myself to shift in this way, I feel . . . Inhale . . . exhale . . .

Emit   HUM three to five times, transforming reactions such as controlling into shifting.

Activate   See it! Visualize an image of shift, perhaps a shift in the ocean tide or season, or you may imagine the yellow ray of light.

Nourish   Feel it! Relax your body. Sense and feel a ray of light. Allow the ray to fill you up with energy, allowing this internal change to happen with ease and noneffort. As you fill up, the ray naturally pours into your environment and into Mother Earth so all beings can gain the inner strength to create shifts.

Surrender   Say: *I allow change. I allow shifting. I allow freshness. I allow freedom.*

Ease   Say: *I am change. I am shifting. I am aware. I am conscious. I am free.*

Cleansing for Confidence

When my husband came home and told me his company had cut our family's insurance, I responded with a sigh. Although he had a pretty good attitude about the situation—"I'll find a new job,"he said—part of me wondered what we were in for. You may have expected this section to be about confidence in yourself, and certainly this is important, yet in this Cleanse you are learning how to be confident in your attractions.

An attraction can be a set of circumstances, a change in direction, a person who shows up in your life, and more. The question is: How will you gain the confidence that this is truly happening for you? By now you may know the answer is to Cleanse. You see, when I sat down to do this, I realized I had a real opportunity here. You know how many people don't feel secure in their circumstances—individuals and families who depend on services like child support, medical benefits, insurance coverage, and so forth? Once you realize your attractions have a greater purpose, you will have no problem embracing them in your life. Remember: what you resist, constricts. You always have a choice; that will never change. See all attractions as happening for you. By the way, although there were moments of great discomfort, in the end, leaving that job ended up being the best attraction for our family!

Clear Reactivity　Pour a glass of water, sit down for moment, and allow yourself to take some small sips. Pay attention to the way you swallow the water. So often we can chug something down mindlessly. Both hydrating and swallowing are great for toning your vagus nerve, reassuring it that it is safe to feel. After a few mindful sips, move to the next step.

Look Inward　*How I feel in my body right now is* . . . Inhale . . . exhale . . .

Having this attraction show up in my life this way now makes me feel . . . Inhale . . . exhale . . .

Having the stamina and energy to trust what is in the works now makes me feel . . . Inhale . . . exhale . . .

Emit HUM three to five times, tapping the roof of your mouth with your tongue. Release and transform anxiety into confidence.

Activate See it! Visualize an image of calm and secure, perhaps a peaceful ocean, or imagine the yellow ray of light.

Nourish Shower the ray of yellow light onto your image. Allow it to saturate Mother Earth so anyone on this planet with similar fears, reactions, or concerns can receive these vibrations of confidence, reassurance, and resiliency.

Surrender Say: *I allow confidence. I allow reassurance. I allow resilience. I allow freedom.*

Ease Say: *I am confidence. I am reassurance. I am resilient. I am free.*

MANIFESTING MESSAGE

If you want to increase something in your life, such as money, love, better health, or good grades, then you are going to want to focus on increasing circulation. In other words, if you want to increase customer sales in your business, then you want your product or service to be circulated. One way to nourish this intention is to *notice, observe, allow, and receive* opportunities to cultivate circulation. It can be as simple as moving energy through your body by breathing or taking time to be truly present to another. Connection is one of the best ways to increase circulation. It feels so good to be connected to one another—it is like food for the soul. I once had a client who wanted to get high marks on an exam so she could get a promotion. The high marks was her goal, yet what would fuel the goal would be her intention. Together we set the intention to keep things light and remember to have fun. Fun, laughter, and playfulness are wonderful creative energies. Sure, study for the test, yet it is important not to minimize the power of energy when it is in flow.

Affirmation: I attract meaningful experiences into my life now.

CHAPTER 8

The Law of Detachment

Tune in to this law to . . .
Relinquish and let go. Transform fear and doubt.
Bring in peace.

The Law of Detachment states that in order to manifest our desires, we must release attachment to the outcome itself as well as the path we might take to get there." That's what Sarah Regan wrote on the MindBodyGreen website. In other words, if you want success, love, or support, you need to detach from the way you believe it ought to happen. When in doubt, detach. Yet as you can imagine, that can be easier said than done. Cleansing and getting to know this law can help.

Here is the thing: when you are in a state of attachment, there is likely a lot of ego energy present. The ego energy functions similar to a defensive mechanism. It has a lot of pride. It is the part of you that doesn't want to look bad, fail, or be alone. As a result, you may attempt to protect yourself. You may pretend you are fine, go into fearful thinking, quit, analyze, or pick apart a situation. In other words, your decision making and thoughts are being pushed by fear. To push is pressure. This is not energy in action; this is a reaction—a state of suffering.

When you are in a state of detachment, you feel more at ease. You are allowing yourself to experience everything (highs, lows, ups, downs) without getting attached (believing) to the thoughts that come your way. This is because you recognize triggered thoughts, which are often memories of the past or projections of the future. A state of detachment exists in the present—the same state in which you can *notice, observe, allow, and receive.*

One of the ways to align yourself with the Law of Detachment is to reassess what you value. You see, when you attach to things, like an outcome, money, or even the need to know how things will turn out, you weaken your vibration, and this causes you to become preoccupied, consumed, and in some cases, obsessed with things, situations, and circumstances out of your control. For example, you may value freedom and your spare time, yet you tend to overwork yourself. You work hard to gain more free time. Here is the thing: if you don't value the time you have, then how are you going to attract more of it? If you value love, then why not love more of yourself? If you value abundance, then consider tuning in to the areas of your life where it exists. In other words, let your values shift your thinking rather than your thinking develop your values.

The Law of Detachment encourages you to loosen your grip, relax a little bit, and let go of the need to do, be, or work harder. Taking an inventory now and then of what you value (time, love, affection, space, fun) can help you realign yourself with this law.

You are disconnected from this law when . . .

○ You are fixed on a certain outcome or problem.
○ You give others or yourself ultimatums.
○ You feel territorial or easily offended.
○ You believe other people are inconsiderate of your wants or needs.
○ You feel separate or alone, maybe even wounded by someone choosing to disconnect from you.
○ You cling to the past or worry about the future.
○ You are in a trigger state, perhaps talking, thinking, or ranting about the things you dislike or can't have.
○ You are holding yourself back from saying something inappropriate or angry.

You are connected to this law when . . .

- You let go of controlling other people's journeys.
- You honor your emotions by breathing and taking some space for yourself.
- You have a sense of inner strength.
- You are able to be the observer or the witness rather than attach to thoughts.
- You are grateful for the lessons even if they came with discomfort and pain.
- You no longer feel the need to defend your position. You are able to respond clearly without getting heated.
- You feel calm and secure.
- You are no longer pushing through your pain; instead, you take your foot off the gas pedal and allow yourself to ride out the discomfort.
- You give permission to others to do what feels right (even if you don't agree).
- You accept the reactions of another without needing to change them.
- You choose to love and honor your emotions.

CORRESPONDING RAY OF LIGHT: PINK

The pink ray is all about love, beauty, patience, creativity, and self-compassion. It is a wonderful ray to call upon when you are looking to create peaceful resolution and relationships. When it shows up, it often has a soothing, warm, and calming effect on your body. However, the pink ray also has the power to open your heart, which can make you feel vulnerable sometimes. I always say pink can sometimes make you feel like you need to cry, yet you can't—not because you don't want to but rather because you are in a state tipped so far toward love. This is the state from which empathy, compassion, and forgiveness arise. If you find yourself having a tough time letting things go, if you are holding onto past resentments, or if the situation you are going through requires more patience, the pink ray is here to help.

THE LAW OF DETACHMENT: COMPANION CLEANSES

Cleansing for Surrender

When you are in a state of detachment, you are surrendering your thoughts, fears, and defensive mechanisms to something greater. This may be your creator or the god of your understanding. Even if you are unsure what you believe, the rays of light are all-encompassing. When you sense their presence, you are picking up on the higher vibrations of unconditional love, compassion, and patience they carry. When we attempt to solve things from a physical (human) level without being connected to something greater, the ego energy gets activated, and this rears up old defensive mechanisms. Surrender is your way of trusting and honoring that there has got to be a better way than this. Think of the ego energy as a mosquito; it is annoying and can be painful, yet it really doesn't have power over you. This is an illusion. You don't have to figure everything out on your own; the laws, spiritual masters, and guides can assist you. All you have to do is open yourself up to the rays of light!

Clear Reactivity   Take a moment now to sit or stand up tall. Reach your arms overhead and stretch side to side a few times. Release your arms down by your sides, observe your inhale, and exhale.

Look Inward   *How I feel in my body right now is* . . . Inhale . . . exhale . . . *Now that I am opening to surrender, I feel* . . . Inhale . . . exhale . . . *Detaching from the details and outcome now makes me feel* . . . Inhale . . . exhale . . .

Emit   HUM three to five times (nice and slow).

Activate   See it! Visualize an image of liberation, surrender, and freedom, perhaps water releasing from a dam. Or imagine the pink ray of light streaming down on you now.

Nourish   Feel it! Tune in to the pink ray of light. Allow this ray to fill you up with beauty. Concentrate on opening your field of energy beyond your physical body so people miles away can receive the peaceful presence of this pink ray of light.

Surrender   Say: *I allow detachment. I allow patience. I allow peace. I allow freedom.*

Ease   Say: *I am detachment. I am patience. I am liberated. I am ease. I am free.*

Cleansing for Inner Strength

Maryanne had been going through fertility treatment for years. The medical process had been long, and she described it as an emotional roller coaster. Yet this was not the first time Maryanne had that feeling in her body. As a child, she had been diagnosed with body dysmorphia. When I was working with Maryanne, the Law of Detachment was one of the laws she was having difficulty grasping. Because her diagnosis required quite a bit of monitoring (meditations and therapy) and her fertility process was taking its toll, she came to me looking for help learning how to process her feelings.

Through Cleansing, we discovered that her preoccupation with her physical appearance as an adolescent attached her to certain ideas, stories, and narratives. Although her health had improved as an adult, now she found herself in a similar situation; only instead of attaching to numbers on a scale, it was to results of treatment outcomes. Through this Cleanse, she was able to process (move the energy) an earlier event in her life to support a current situation. It was her energy in action that allowed her to build the inner strength she needed to foster vibrations of self-love and acceptance.

Clear Reactivity   Roll your shoulders around several times, loosening any tension in your neck. Then take one deep breath through your nose, and on an exhale, open your mouth and make the AHH sound three times.

Look Inward   *How I feel in my body right now is* . . . Inhale . . . exhale . . .

And when I measure, compare, or get caught up in the details, I feel . . . Inhale . . . exhale . . .

Discovering this newfound inner strength makes me feel . . . Inhale . . . exhale . . .

And when I focus on my internal space, I feel . . . Inhale . . . exhale . . .

Emit   HUM three to five times.

Activate   See it! Visualize wholeness, perhaps the sun. Or imagine the pink ray of light.

Nourish   Feel it! Saturate yourself in the pink ray. Allow the pink ray's download frequencies of peace, patience, and compassion.

Surrender   Say: *I allow inner strength. I allow trust. I allow space. I allow self-compassion.*

Ease   Say: *I am faith. I am compassion. I am whole. I am self-compassion.*

Cleansing for Honor

Tom let me know he had a stressful week and that he was working hard at keeping his emotions in check. He said, "Inside I am really pissed off, but I am doing everything I can to not say anything that would get me in trouble." What you don't know about Tom is he had a temper. He was aware he could blow up and tried his best to restrain himself by walking away or going for a ride in his car. Yet neither of these strategies really helped him move the energy of his anger in a productive way. In fact, when he reentered his home or workplace after walking away, he admitted (during a Cleanse) that he often felt embarrassed and ashamed. He told me this was similar to how he felt in school as a kid.

As he was speaking, I could sense the pink ray of light coming in. This is what is so amazing to me about the rays. Once you get a relationship with them, they begin to effortlessly show up during times of need. The truth of the matter is Tom was beginning to move the anger (via the Cleanse). We walked through the steps together, and as this pent-up energy gained motion, it lifted just enough so we could experience the calming presence of the pink ray.

When you give yourself permission, you can feel states of detachment arise. This is the way it works; just be open, honest, and willing.

Clear Reactivity   Scoot yourself forward to the front of your chair (or stand up), and interlace your hands behind your back, giving yourself a gentle stretch in the front of your chest. Hold this for about one minute, release your hands, and take an inhale and exhale.

Look Inward   *How I feel in my body right now is* . . . Inhale . . . exhale . . .

Honoring my emotions in this way makes me feel . . . Inhale . . . exhale . . .

When I respect and value what I am feeling, I feel . . . Inhale . . . exhale . . .

Releasing the need to control or contain my emotions now makes me feel . . . Inhale . . . exhale . . .

Emit   HUM three to five times.

Activate   See it! Visualize an image of release, perhaps an ocean's tide or dandelions floating through the air. What do you see? Activate the pink ray in your imagination.

Nourish   Feel it! Now receive the peaceful, compassionate rays of pink light. Fill yourself up and allow this feeling to spill over into the lives of others.

Surrender   Say: *I allow release. I allow respect. I allow honor. I allow love. I allow freedom.*

Ease   Say: *I am respect. I am honor. I am feeling. I am free.*

Cleansing for Relief

Have you ever been invited somewhere with a friend and there was a part of you that expected you were not going to have a fun time? Or perhaps you were preparing to go on vacation and started thinking (expecting) how much worse you're going to look on the beach compared to everyone else? Or maybe you relate to expectations in terms of putting pressure on yourself.

Here is the thing: expectations deflate your energy, big time. It is like blowing up a balloon all the way and sticking a pin in it. Then you have to cope with the feeling of being deflated, which could, without your awareness, be some unprocessed emotions of embarrassment, guilt, or shame. When it comes to the Law of Detachment, it is important that you release (transform) these expectations, otherwise you can set yourself up for feeling disappointed (which by the way really isn't a feeling; it is a reaction). It will only hinder your ability to trust the signs and signals that come your way, not to mention your self-esteem.

Clear Reactivity   Take a moment to sit down, and if possible, kick off your socks and shoes so you can rub (massage) the tops of your feet. There are places (acupressure points) on your feet that connect with the energy of your body. Notice how when you rub the tops or bottoms of your feet, your abdominals soften, loosening any stress in that area. Do this for about a minute, and then move to the next step.

Look Inward   *How I feel in my body right now is* . . . Inhale . . . exhale . . .

Now that I am opening to loosening expectations, I feel . . . Inhale . . . exhale . . .

Transforming pressure into peace now makes me feel. . . Inhale . . . exhale . . .

Emit   HUM three to five times or more. On the last HUM, extend it with one long breath (on the exhale).

Activate   See it! Imagine an image of comfort, relief, calm, and free, perhaps an image of soaking your feet in warm salt water. Filter in the pink ray.

Nourish   Bathe in the light. Allow it to transform all your negative, critical thoughts into gentle, kind, beautiful words. May anyone who is carrying the reaction of expecting loss, sadness, or lack benefit from these beautiful rays as you connect them to the planet.

Surrender   Say: *I allow release. I allow detachment. I allow beautiful thoughts.*

Ease   Say: *I am detachment. I am relief. I am kindness. I am free.*

MANIFESTING MESSAGE

If you want to remove negativity in your life, then your intention will be to focus on freedom. Negativity (whether it is yours or someone else's) may be a sign of feeling restricted. You need space to detach. Just like a plant requires space to grow, you may benefit from space to enhance your ability to notice, observe, allow, and receive freedom. Ask yourself if there are tasks, roles, or habits you can relinquish. Are there areas you may be overdoing it? How might detaching from expectations and outcomes support your inner freedom?

Affirmation: I let go and allow.

CHAPTER 9

The Law of Cause and Effect

Tune in to this law to . . .
Increase progress. Transform comparisons.
Support boundaries.

This law states that every action has a companion reaction. In other words, every action you take has a ripple effect, even if you don't see it right away. For example, let's say you have a fight with your partner and blow off some steam by saying hurtful things before you march out of the room. This action not only impacts your partner but also has an effect on you. You may feel the impact later and find yourself struggling with fatigue, anxiety, guilt, or frustration. You may think, *That is because we had a fight, and I was stressed.* While that may be true, it can also be a sign you are affected by what happened. In the moment, it might have felt good to let some things off your chest, but now you are in a state of suffering.

Focusing on your losses, conflicts, or struggles will cause a ripple in your field of energy. It's similar to how after throwing a pebble in a pond of water, rings begin rippling outward. One way to counter these tendencies is to take time to acknowledge your wins: What is going well for you? What have you received from the situation? Is there something you are learning about yourself? What are you grateful for? The answers to these questions are your wins. You may be surprised to see how many good things can come from a negative or traumatic situation.

The Law of Cause and Effect reminds us to always take time to notice the good. This produces a strong movement of energy, transforming any patterns of behavior that showed up. When you process (move) the energy and tune in to higher wisdom, you are able to see how you can consciously choose to ripple energy. This will always override anything fearful or negative.

You are disconnected from this law when . . .

○ You are stuck in a problem or ruminating on your thoughts.
○ You are judging something as good or bad.
○ You are focused on your losses.
○ You ask questions like: What did I do? Do you think it will work out?
○ You feel like things are your fault or you did something wrong.
○ You fantasize something bad will happen (perhaps you have ill-will toward someone).
○ You worry your negative thoughts will cause bad things to come.

You are connected to this law when . . .

○ You connect to your body and your breath.
○ You take time to notice what you have received (there is always something).
○ You are patient.
○ You notice the magnificence in others and in your day.
○ You no longer base decisions predominately on past experiences.
○ You notice the positive impact of simple, small acts or changes.
○ You forgive or have compassion for yourself.
○ You notice the good in yourself and others.

CORRESPONDING RAY OF LIGHT: ORANGE

The orange ray, like the green ray, is about healing, abundance, and miracles. It helps clear things on both a soul level and a subconscious level. It helps you to get to the root of the problem as it can transform systems, patterns, and reactions that may have come from another lifetime. If you have trouble connecting to it, consider putting your attention on something that is orange—a sunrise, piece of fruit, or flower. Remember, allowing your intentions and emotions to flow is how you develop a strong connection to these rays.

THE LAW OF CAUSE AND EFFECT: COMPANION CLEANSES

Cleansing for Value

Sandy's father died when she was a little girl, and she managed this tragedy by telling herself that it was her fault. A few times Sandy didn't do what she was told or gave her dad a hard time, and somehow, she twisted these incidences into a story that she contributed to the stress that caused her father's heart to stop. You may relate to wondering if you had responded differently to a particular situation, whether the outcome would have been different.

While you can't go back in time, what you can do is transform the emotions that seem to replay these feelings. Very often the root of the imbalances with the Law of Cause and Effect are unprocessed emotions of regret, shame, and guilt. Without realizing it, these suppressed emotions can make life seem unmanageable, overwhelming, and difficult. Turning to the orange ray will help relieve you of these burdens so you can transform any beliefs that support this pattern.

Clear Reactivity　　Sit up tall in a comfortable seated position. With your two "peace-sign" fingers on your dominant hand, gently press above your navel (about an inch above your navel, with your fingers about one inch apart). Do three presses. Place the other hand on the back of your neck, near the base of your skull. Use your peace fingers on that hand to press the back of your neck while moving the bottom hand. Press for a count of three in both areas. Repeat two or three times. Release and observe your breath for five seconds.

Look Inward　　*How I feel in my body right now is* . . . Inhale . . . exhale . . .

Giving myself permission to move this energy now makes me feel . . .
Inhale . . . exhale . . .

Transforming fault into freedom now makes me feel . . . Inhale . . .
exhale . . .

Emit   HUM three to five times, releasing and transforming.

Activate   See it! Visualize an image of a beautiful old tree with the glow of the orange ray behind it.

Nourish   Feel it! The orange ray can be very grounding. It runs deep into our inner root system, providing healing on a soul and subconscious level.

Surrender   Say: *I allow unconditional love. I allow admiration. I allow deep soul and subconscious healing. I allow value.*

Ease   Say: *I am presence. I am healing. I am grounding. I am free.*

Cleansing for Opportunity

Let me ask you this: If you were around a few negative people, perhaps they were bitching and complaining about their jobs, politics, or life itself, how would being around this energy affect you? Maybe you would be fine for a little while, but if it occurred often, my guess is over time you might feel irritated, frustrated, and uneasy. Here is the thing: "Negative" people and energy can no doubt take a toll on you. Before you know it, you start to see these individuals or situations as potential problems, obstacles, or barriers to the life you are looking to create.

When working with the Spiritual Law of Cause and Effect, it is important not to confuse obstacles with reactions. In other words, is seeing the other person or situation as "negative" a way of managing what you feel? If it is, then you haven't shifted your inner movement. So in essence, your reaction is still having an effect on your life (even if you are separated from the things or people that you felt were zapping your energy).

While setting personal boundaries, it is important not to do so to get away from the person or situation (as that is a reaction).

Instead, give purpose to your boundaries. Set them as a way to support your intentions of *noticing, observing, allowing, and receiving.* Do you see the difference? Once you learn how to do this, it really supports your ability to be in alignment with this law.

Clear Reactivity Sit up tall in a comfortable seated position. Take your right arm across the front of your body (and chest), giving yourself a gentle shoulder stretch. You may press your arm gently toward you with your left hand to support the stretch. Release and repeat on the other side. Take you left arm across your body, stretching your left shoulder. Release, inhale, and exhale fully.

Look Inward *How I feel in my body right now is . . .* Inhale . . . exhale . . .

Creating boundaries in this way makes me feel . . . Inhale . . . exhale . . .

Having this opportunity to align with my intentions makes me feel . . . Inhale . . . exhale . . .

Emit HUM three to five times to release and transform negativity into opportunity.

Activate See it! Visualize the orange ray of light. Observe it above you, around you, within, and below you.

Nourish Feel it! Sense the filter of the orange ray as it transmutes all negativity. Share this experience with Mother Earth by letting go of any resistance, softening, relaxing, and breathing.

Surrender Say: *I allow opening. I allow opportunities. I allow expansion. I allow freedom.*

Ease Say: *I am healing. I am open. I am abundance. I am free.*

Cleansing for Exploration

To explore means to go beyond fixed mindsets. Give yourself permission to ask questions and learn more before making your decisions. When you feel rushed or pushed in a certain direction, I encourage you to pause, as acting on impulse can contract (rather than expand) energy. Contracted energy can make you feel rushed or panicky. The Law of Cause and Effect is here to guide you, not prevent you. Sometimes you may feel like you are working against yourself, which is the cause of your own suffering.

The Law of Cause and Effect encourages you to explore but not necessarily your thoughts or mind. One way to align with this law is to ask more questions. I love asking questions because they really open up the flow of energy—even simple questions, such as, How was your weekend? Very often when I work with clients, I begin by asking them questions such as this. To an observer, it may seem like I am chit-chatting, but as an energy practitioner, I am consciously choosing to open the conversation to get the energy moving. It is almost as if I let the energy do the work for me. This is what it looks like to work with the laws. As long as it is conscious and includes the four intentions of *noticing, observing, allowing, and receiving*, you will be able to see how the energy in action does the work for you.

Once you ask the question, practice listening and tuning in to the response by practicing the four intentions of energy. A good place to start is to practice on things or situations that have less of a charge in your life. For example, ask what kind of flower you are looking at and explore the feedback through the four intentions. Notice the ripple (cause and affect) without judgment.

Clear Reactivity   Sit up tall in a comfortable seated position. Roll your shoulders back and down and relax your jaw, bringing your chin parallel to the earth. In a moment, you are going to chant the mantra YAM. YAM is the seed sound for the heart chakra. Chakras are areas of the body where energy pools and circulates. As you chant the sound YAM ten to twenty times, the energy around the heart center will vibrate and circulate. After twenty times, pause and feel the energy. Breathe naturally. If you desire, you may continue for twenty more times or move to step two. Do what feels right, knowing this Cleanse is always here for you.

Look Inward   *How I feel in my body right now is* . . . Inhale . . . exhale . . .

Asking questions makes me feel . . . Inhale . . . exhale . . .

When I let the energy do the work, I feel . . . Inhale . . . exhale . . .

Living life in this way now makes me feel . . . Inhale . . . exhale . . .

Emit   HUM three to five times, allowing the orange ray of light to work effortlessly through you.

Activate   See it! Visualize the orange ray of light moving freely within the space between you and another.

Nourish   Feel it! Pour the ray of orange light into the atmosphere, loosening the energy of disconnection on the planet. May all souls benefit from this process.

Surrender   Say: *I allow exploration. I allow soul cleansing. I allow freedom.*

Ease   Say: *I am exploration. I am soul cleansing. I am liberated. I am free.*

Cleansing for Action

There may be times in your life when you are frustrated or even disappointed by your progress. Perhaps you had hoped to be further along by now. This may cause you to question your decision to move in this direction in the first place. Is this really the right relationship for you? Maybe you should have chosen a different career path? Or perhaps the school you are attending isn't the right fit? If the Spiritual Law of Cause and Effect could speak, it would say, *Stop trying so hard.*

You see, all that trying (problem solving, pressure, figuring things out) can take up quite a bit of energy. You want action, movement, and progress, but all that trying constricts movement. Again, the Law of Cause and Effect is all about the ripple.

Here is the thing that I think you ought to know: not all action happens in the physical realm. This means that just because you don't see it, doesn't mean it isn't in the works. If you are rippling movement, assume it is all happening. The moment you doubt or quit listening to your gut (intuition), you are holding back the ripple. This is not bad or wrong; it just appears as if your life is not working when it is!

In other words, you don't always have to do something. This is an unconscious habit based on fear. When things aren't happening on the outside, turn inward and realign with the intentions of *noticing, observing, allowing, and receiving.* All these intentions ripple outward (similar to an ocean tide) and return to you, with new solutions, ideas, and ways of approaching things. You have got this!

Clear Reactivity   Sit up nice and tall in a comfortable seated position. Tilt your chin slightly upward (as if you were gargling) and make the AHH sound. The point is to create some movement in your throat area. Do this a few times and then move to the next step.

Look Inward   *How I feel in my body right now is . . .* Inhale . . . exhale . . .

When energy is in action, I feel . . . Inhale . . . exhale . . .

Rippling energy makes me feel . . . Inhale . . . exhale . . .

Emit   HUM three to five times.

Activate   See it! Imagine the movement of the orange ray. See the orange ray expand inside of you when you inhale, and on the exhale, imagine the orange ray filling up your aura.

Nourish   Feel it! Notice the grounding effect. Allow it to nurture the soul of Mother Earth.

Surrender   Say: *I allow grounding. I allow action. I allow movement. I allow freedom.*

Ease   Say: *I am action. I am solutions. I am focused. I am free.*

MANIFESTING MESSAGE

When you find yourself over-focusing on what you are upset about, whether it be a person or a situation, you are mindlessly giving your energy away. This can have a direct impact on your life. I once had a client who was so over-focused on how much she needed to break up with her boyfriend that she neglected to see how this was impacting other areas of her life. For example, her home and her car were a mess. She would often complain about how much she had to do. I remember asking her, "Have you noticed the way over-focusing on him impacts your life? Have you noticed how giving him so much attention depletes your energy? As a result, you have little motivation, desire, or energy to take care of your own life." The point was to help her see the connection to the spiritual law of cause and effect. Notice how the law of cause and effect may be impacting your life. If you want a healthy relationship, then you will want to decrease distractibility. Practice noticing and observing by taking time to be more present in the here and now.

Affirmation: I choose light.

CHAPTER 10

The Law of Correspondence

Tune in to this law to . . .
Transform a pattern. Regain your power.
Honor your reflections.

The Law of Correspondence states that our outer world reflects our inner world. In other words, what you see on the outside reflects (the energy) on the inside. This law reminds us that there is no separation: what is outside of you is inside of you, and vice versa. New Thought leaders, such as Wayne Dyer, Epictetus, and James Allen, captured this law perfectly when they said, "Circumstances do not make a man; they reveal him."

You see, you are more than physical anatomy. You are more than your organs, blood, and physical features. You are energy. Energy has movement and nonmovement. The more you react to what you see on the outside, the less movement you will have on the inside. I often use the term "movement systems." These systems, when repeated, create *patterns*. Therefore, what you see on the outside may reflect a pattern of reactivity on the inside. Very often, we see this in relationships. People draw certain individuals into their lives not necessarily because they have a lot in common (on the outside) but most likely because they carry a similar pattern of energy.

It is always fascinating to me how two people can have the same exact pattern (for example, a controlling feeling) but react in opposite ways. For example, one person may be super responsible and do everything perfectly, and another person may be completely irresponsible, unpredictable, and erratic. One manages their fears by trying to manage the behaviors of the person in front of them (for example, by doing things for them), while another manages by pushing people away (such as by picking fights). Same control system, different behaviors. Each is reflecting the same inner world (feeling out of control) even though it may look different on the outside.

The Law of Correspondence helps you honor your attractions rather than judge them. I know we don't like to think about how these patterns exist inside of us, yet you need to know that your patterns are not who you really are. You are a spiritual being having a human experience. The rays are not separate from you; they are you. You, as a spirit, are these vibrations (of love, peace, compassion, and so forth). If you are having a hard time believing this, cultivating a relationship with the blue ray of light will help.

You are disconnected from this law when . . .

- You overextend yourself or are juggling many things at once.
- You hold onto old hurts and resentments.
- You say things like, "Why me?"
- You feel pressured or panicky about a decision.
- You act on impulse. For example, you might send a quick text and regret it later.
- You judge or rant about what is most on your mind.
- You distance or cut yourself off from others.
- You feel powerless.
- You expected something and did not get it.
- You protect or prevent vulnerability.

You are connected to this law when . . .

- You are able to make a connection between an emotional trigger and a pattern.
- You are able to own your attractions without judgment.
- You are open to learning more.
- You see yourself as connected to something greater.
- You see reflections as opportunities to move energy.
- You communicate your needs after you take time to process your emotions.

○ You feel humble, open, and vulnerable.

○ You notice your choices.

CORRESPONDING RAY OF LIGHT: BLUE

If you are feeling powerless, unprotected, or devalued, the blue ray is an incredible ray to connect with. The blue ray removes all illusion so your self-awareness and divine love can shine through. The blue ray has strong attributes of faith, true power, and wisdom. It can be difficult to face or accept some situations, yet the blue ray reminds you that you are not alone, to surrender, and to let go of illusion.

If this ray could be described in four words, they would be: *protection, love, spiritual wisdom.* I often experience it as a cool temperature, and those I have worked with describe this ray as an experience of inner space. The blue ray allows you to take in the big picture and clear negative thinking as you develop protection and strength.

THE LAW OF CORRESPONDENCE: COMPANION CLEANSES

Cleansing for Harmony

Albert Einstein taught us you can't solve a problem by being in it. You have to go outside the problem and learn how to become the observer. This is an important skill for you to develop as you learn how to live harmoniously with this law. This can be difficult if you are judging, comparing, and contrasting the people and situations in your life.

For example, I once worked with someone who talked about how she felt much further along in her spiritual development than her partner. She would say things like, "Well, that is because I have done more work on myself." While she may truly have believed she was in a different place and mindset than her partner, the fact that she was managing what she felt by comparing and contrasting herself indicated she was out of alignment with this law. In other words, she saw her partner as separate from herself, as if they were on two different paths. Yet, through Cleansing, it was revealed that she and her partner tended to manage their emotions by overthinking and extending themselves. This can happen in relationships, yet when things get so intertwined, it can be difficult to see that the two of you are one and the same. The blue ray downloads vibrations of protection so you are able to stay strong in who you are. Nevermind what everyone else is doing or the ways they are growing (or not).

Clear Reactivity   In this centering exercise, you will do a breath technique called left-nostril breathing. The intention is to bring a calming sensation to your nervous system. Sit up tall in a comfortable seated position. With your thumb, close your right nostril and inhale slowly through your left for a count of four as you inflate your abdomen. Keeping your right nostril closed, exhale through your left, pulling your navel toward your spine, again for the count of four. Really sink into your exhale. Repeat this two or three times.

Look Inward   *How I feel in my body right now is* . . . Inhale . . . exhale . . .

Recognizing these patterns in me makes me feel . . . Inhale . . . exhale . . .

Now that I am open to embracing these reflections, I feel . . . Inhale . . . exhale . . .

Emit   HUM three to five times, tapping the roof of your mouth with your tongue. After your last HUM, pause and observe your breathing for a few seconds.

Activate   See it! Imagine harmony, perhaps an orchestra of instruments creating a new rhythm and beat. Visualize the blue ray of light.

Nourish   Receive the protective vibrations of the blue ray of light. Know that these protective vibrations reflect the faith, power, and protection inside of you.

Surrender   Say: *I allow faith. I allow true power. I allow protection. I allow freedom.*

Ease   Say: *I am faith. I am true power. I am eternal freedom. I am protection.*

Cleansing for Humility

Not many people like the idea of vulnerability. This is because they associate it with being susceptible to hurt, disappointment, and pain. Yet without vulnerability, it can be difficult to foster trust and connection. You see, it is vulnerability that allows the other person to witness both your strengths and areas you are developing. Vulnerability is what keeps things real and raw. Yet sometimes vulnerability can be covered up by an unhealthy sense of pride. This is what causes people to go back on their word, keep their guard up, or have a copious amount of vanity. Through Cleansing, I have found that these behaviors can sometimes be a way of managing emotions of shame.

If you are finding yourself taking things personally, keeping your guard up, or feeling like you are better (or further along) than someone else, you are slowing down the energy. There is no "better than" spirit; it just is. If I think I am doing better, then a part of me doesn't want to see how what I am judging in another is also in me. Think of it like a Band-Aid: Is it better to pull it off quickly or take it off slowly? Judgment (ego) is the slow version, while feeling, or intuition, gets you right to the source. You don't have to dwell in it, and you don't even have to like it, but you do want to consciously choose to move the energy that is showing up (and then download) and connect to a ray of light.

The blue ray gives a sense of security and shelter when something seems impossible. Trust.

Clear Reactivity   Sit up tall in a comfortable position. Close your eyes and slowly inhale through your nose (inflating the sides of your waist), and then on the exhale, open your mouth, letting out an AHH sound while pulling your navel toward your spine. Repeat this two or three times.

Look Inward   *How I feel in my body right now is* . . . Inhale . . . exhale . . .

Letting go of all judgments now makes me feel . . . Inhale . . . exhale . . .

Being vulnerable makes me feel . . . Inhale . . . exhale . . .

Allowing the blue ray of light to move through me now makes me feel . . . Inhale . . . exhale . . .

Emit   HUM three to five times, releasing the illusion of separation.

Activate   See it! Visualize the blue ray of light streaming down on you through the crown of your head, through the central channel of your body, through your core, and out the soles of your feet.

Nourish   Feel it! Allow the blue ray of light to embody you and Mother Earth. May anyone else on the planet who needs protection and faith benefit.

Surrender   Say: *I allow protection. I allow honor. I allow self-respect. I allow freedom.*

Ease   Say: *I am allowing. I am honor. I am trust. I am protected. I am free.*

Cleansing for True Power

One of the biggest misconceptions that gets in the way of people's manifesting ability is the way in which they interpret power. If you see power as something outside of you, then you have likely been misled. You are not alone. So many people view power as control. They see other people who are in situations or positions of power, and this makes them feel powerless. To be a true manifester, you must know that power is inside of you. This Cleanse will help. I once asked someone during a Cleanse what their visualization of true power was. Their response was, "I don't know, all I see is an image of stars in the sky, and I feel like one of them." "Go with that image," I responded. After the Cleanses, I encouraged her to take what she learned and apply it. I suggested she go outside (or look out a window at the night sky) every night for the next seven days to remind herself what true power is. True power makes you feel (not think) like you are part of something greater. Be the stars, be the sky, be the sun, be the tree; this is true power.

Clear Reactivity   Sit up tall in a comfortable position. Let yourself do an imaginary yawn. Perhaps stretch your arms overhead as you do this. Release and roll your shoulders up, back, and down.

Look Inward   *How I feel in my body right now is* . . . Inhale . . . exhale . . .

Acknowledging my true power makes me feel . . . Inhale . . . exhale . . .

Having this insight about myself makes me feel . . . Inhale . . . exhale . . .

Emit   HUM three to five times, clearing and transforming any false perceptions about power.

Activate   See it! Visualize the stars in the sky or whatever else comes to you. What makes you feel powerful? Be it. See it.

Nourish   Feel it! Bask in a ray of blue light, immersing yourself in the vibrations of true power, faith, and creativity. Allow this energy to generously flow through you. May all beings receive the blessing of true power.

Surrender   Say: *I allow true power. I allow connection. I allow unity. I allow freedom.*

Ease   Say: *I am true power. I am connection. I am unity. I am free.*

Cleansing for Grace

There are times in life when you may feel surrounded by individuals who are in high levels of reactivity, perhaps people behaving in ways that are not just hurtful but also manipulative and even possibly corrupt. If you are feeling bullied, intimidated, or even abused, in addition to getting help, confide in someone you trust, letting them know what is going on. Supplement these supports with the Cleanse and the blue ray of light.

A state of grace comes with ease. Archangel Michael seems to be one of the most consistent spiritual masters connected to this ray.

When the blue ray is around, you feel invincible. Nothing, and I mean nothing, can get in your way.

The Law of Correspondence reminds us that what we see on the outside is a reflection of what is on the inside. If you feel intimated (bullied), there might be an aspect of you that believes you are smaller, weaker, or powerless. I have worked with people who have been bullied and were perpetrators of bullying. At the core level, they both carry the same inner movement. In other words, the pattern of energy is experienced in the body very similarly. I once asked someone who bullied what it felt like in her body when she behaved that way, and she said it felt tight and clogged. I have asked people who had been bullied, and they reported a similar energetic experience.

Once you see that everything is about energy in action (or inaction), you stop focusing on pain, and you start to pay more attention to movement. The blue ray builds you up with protective energy, and as a result you feel strong, steady, and focused. Grace is the ability to maintain your stability during times when things on the outside may appear chaotic. Align with this law by calling on the blue ray of light and ask for assistance from those, such as Archangel Michael, who oversee it.

Clear Reactivity Take a deep breath and move your body in whatever way it is looking to be acknowledged. Perhaps stretch your neck, roll your shoulders up and down, or open and close your jaw a few times. Breathe. Once you're settled, move to the next step.

Look Inward *How I feel in my body right now is* . . . Inhale . . . exhale . . .

Now that I am opening to the energy of grace, I feel . . . Inhale . . . exhale . . .

Invoking the blue ray into my life now makes me feel . . . Inhale . . . exhale . . .

Emit HUM three to five times.

Activate See it! Visualize an image of honor, virtue, and integrity, perhaps a bald eagle, which is often a symbol of grace. Or simply imagine and enjoy the blue ray of light.

Nourish Feel it! Marinate in the many hues of the blue ray: light blue, navy blue, cobalt blue, and even aqua.

Surrender Say: *I allow grace. I allow honesty. I allow integrity. I allow freedom.*

Ease Say: *I am protected. I am grace. I am honor. I am free.*

MANIFESTING MESSAGE

You are part of a collective pattern. Patterns can exist through bloodlines and even across lifetimes. All it takes is one person to shift a pattern. Since you are reading this message, you have the capacity. Loosen your grip on the past, because holding on to the past will only inhibit your ability to transform. Allow cycles to come to completion. Some doors will close while others will open. It is not your job to make others happy. It is your job to move energy. When energy is in motion, darkness will dissolve, only to be replaced by the light.

Affirmation: I am an infinite being of light.

CHAPTER 11

The Law of Inspired Action

Tune in to this law . . .
When you feel stuck. For energy and inspiration.
To break a habit.

The Law of Inspired Action is about encouragement. This law nudges you to take small actionable steps toward your dreams and goals. While as much as I would love to tell you sitting in the rays of light is all you need to make changes, that is not true. You do have to take some action.

The Law of Inspired Action supports action. For example, you may be stimulated to travel. Perhaps there is a place you are eager to visit. You may tell yourself that it is not the right time or that it is too much money, yet that feeling you get inside (of inspiration) keeps coming back. You may feel a twinge of nervousness, vulnerability, excitement, or a spark of inner knowing. If you *notice, observe, allow, and receive* this inner movement, you will see how it becomes much easier to take some small, yet meaningful actionable steps.

Should some old fears, anxieties, and beliefs arise, this is where Cleansing can help. Without processing your emotions around this, you might get a little scared and shut the energy down. Remember this: the Spiritual Law of Inspired Action doesn't want to frighten you; it is trying to nudge you (gently). Any actionable steps will do. It can be as simple as making a phone call, looking up a website, or looking at flights.

I once had a client who thought about getting a personal trainer for years before deciding to make the move. Once she did, within a couple of weeks, she had a more positive attitude about her body. After she lost twenty pounds, I decided to ask her how this time felt different. Her response was, "I decided to be kind and loving to myself." She attributed Cleansing, the personal trainer, as well as the choice to have self-love and compassion to her newfound success.

Here is the thing: the Law of Inspired Action will get you out of your comfort zone (in a good way) when you are aligned with it. The key is to build your reservoir of energy up (via Cleansing and rays of light). Before you know it, you will have the courage to make some meaningful changes in your life. Follow your intuition and do what feels right for you.

You are disconnected from this law when . . .

○ You are wondering what your purpose is, beyond raising children and paying the bills.
○ You are longing for love and connection.
○ You feel like you're working hard and getting little to no results.
○ You are hanging on tight (to whatever you believe), waiting for something to shift.
○ You know what steps (habits or changes) you need to make yet are resistant to making them.
○ You feel lost, alone, or unsure.
○ You make decisions out of fear, guilt, or shame.
○ You internalize what you think others believe about you.

You are connected to this law when . . .

○ The sensations (vibration) you gain from processing your emotions become your source of inspiration.
○ You have high levels of commitment in one or a few areas of your life.
○ You have interests or hobbies that bring you to the present moment.
○ You are able to trust that your emotions will open up doorways and provide insight (when processed).
○ You are inspired about ideas, experiences (such as art and travel), and people.

- You quit making excuses, sign up for a class, or go visit a friend.
- You are clear on one action step to take and feel ready and open to taking it.
- You step outside your comfort zone and try things that interest you, while giving yourself permission to move through (transform) some of those uncomfortable feelings.
- You feel alert, and you perk up at certain thoughts or ideas.

CORRESPONDING RAY OF LIGHT: MAGENTA

The magenta ray is about cosmic love. It carries the vibrations of harmony, confidence, divinity, balance, and peace. Its qualities heal generational complications. It can transform inner turmoil, nervousness, and mental and physical imbalances. Some clients have reported different shapes, such as rectangles, showing up in their mind's eye while channeling the magenta ray of light. Shapes and symbols have a sacred geometry and are often used in healing sessions, such as Reiki. Be inspired and motivated by what you see. Let it lift you up so you can access and embody all its amazing qualities. These kinds of happenings represent energy in action.

THE LAW OF INSPIRED ACTION: COMPANION CLEANSES

Cleansing for Purpose

After years of going through a tumultuous divorce, Renee managed to land on her feet. She found a quaint little home, which sat on the base of a mountain, a place where she could go on long walks and spend time in nature. While she was happy with the progress she made, inside she wondered what was next on her journey. Was this her purpose, or was there something more she was meant to do? Through Cleansing, Renee learned that this question was one of the ways she managed her emotions. You see, when she got uncomfortable, unsure, or felt a little lost, the question, What is my purpose? would pop into her mind. During our session, I said, "Your purpose is to feel."

The Law of Inspired Action wants to remind you that you are not an outsider. You are very much part of this gigantic team called the universe. If the Law of Inspired Action could speak, it would say: *Get up off the bench and go play ball. Live your life and quit waiting for the "right time."* Instead of asking yourself, What is my purpose? ask: What moves me? What am I drawn to? What gets me up and off the bench? Notice the answers that come back. Then ask yourself: Does this response really move me, or is this a reaction? How do I know the difference? Be inspired by your own energy (intuition, emotion) in action.

Clear Reactivity   Sit up tall in a comfortable seated position. With one or both of your hands, scratch or massage your head just like you would if you were washing your hair. Do this for about thirty seconds, place your hands on your lap, observe, and breathe.

Look Inward   *How I feel in my body right now is . . .* Inhale . . . exhale . . .

Now that I am getting to know my own source of inspiration, I feel . . . Inhale . . . exhale . . .

Opening myself up to knowing and learning more makes me feel . . . Inhale . . . exhale . . .

Emit   HUM three to five times.

Activate   See it! Imagine the magenta ray of light streaming into your awareness as you visualize yourself taking one or two steps on a pathway. The magenta ray holds you steady and balanced as you make a move.

Nourish   Feel it! Soak up the energy of this magnificent ray. Remember it comes (like you) from a divine loving source.

Surrender   Say: *I allow inspiration. I allow knowing. I allow action. I allow purpose.*

Ease   Say: *I am trust. I am resiliency. I am inner strength. I am free.*

Cleansing for Inspiration

You are your own source of inspiration. Yet if you have been in a situation where something didn't feel right, perhaps you felt someone wasn't being completely honest or transparent with you, this can, without awareness, influence your connection to this vibration. You see, if you are busy trying to figure things out or maybe frame things in such a way so others won't get hurt (and, as a result, don't know what you are really wanting or asking), you slow down your inner energy. When this occurs, you are more likely to miss and perhaps dismiss moments of spontaneous joy. Joy is energy in action. Joy produces inspiration. When these two come together, life becomes tender, sweet, nourishing, and peaceful.

In this Cleanse, I encourage you to take your blinders off and really get grounded so you can tune in to your senses. Allow your sensations to give you the clarity you need to initiate your next steps. It is time to reduce the pressure and go a little easier on yourself by allotting some downtime and remembering that inspiration (movement, change, new beginnings) is in the works.

Clear Reactivity   Take a moment to sit up tall so you can do some deep breathing. Relax your face and jaw and soften your cheek bones, shoulders, hips, and legs. Take a nice slow inhale through your nose, inflating the sides of your waist. On the exhale, pull your navel toward your spine, and squeeze the air out through your nose, nice and slow. Take your time, allowing each breath to be unique. Repeat this two or three times.

Look Inward   *How I feel in my body right now is* . . . Inhale . . . exhale . . .

When I imagine things in my life in action, I feel . . . Inhale . . . exhale . . .

When inspiration is in flow, I feel . . . Inhale . . . exhale . . .

Emit   HUM three to five times, releasing distrust and receiving trust.

Activate   See it! Visualize the magenta ray streaming through an image that makes you feel solid, strong, and confident, such as a mountain or a mustang.

Nourish Feel it! Receive the magenta ray into your being while opening your heart to sharing this experience with Mother Earth. Allow your flow of inspiration to spill over into Mother Earth, supporting the energetic movement of all living beings.

Surrender Say: *I allow inspiration. I allow movement. I allow integrity. I allow trust.*

Ease Say: *I am movement. I am inspiration. I am honor. I am energy. I am free.*

Cleansing for Openness

Have you ever had a time when you missed someone or something? Perhaps you felt an emptiness or longing in your heart. While it might seem like that person or thing would fill the void, it is likely that is an illusion. Here is the challenge: whenever you long or miss something, you're telling the universe that you don't have it or that you are lacking in that area of your life. On the other hand, when you say things like, *I look forward to . . .* , it sends a very different message to the universe. It is not so much about the words; it's that *I look forward to* comes from an open inner space, whereas *I miss* comes from a closed down inner space. Here is the thing: without Cleansing, sometimes these statements can fall flat. While they might sound good, the energy behind them can be weak. If you have been through hardship, pain, or loss, I totally understand why you might be hesitant to get back on your feet (fully) so you can move in a new direction.

I want you to remember that the Law of Inspired Action is doing its best to get your attention. While on the outside it may look like you are moving on or forward, what is really happening is you are going deeper into yourself to discover some things you may have never believed you were capable of—things like love, forgiveness, creativity, and more. Wow, that sounds so inspiring, doesn't it? The Law of Inspired Action is designed to keep you in motion, learning, growing, and contributing to the planet.

Clear Reactivity Center yourself here by imagining you are sitting in the sun. Allow the rays to penetrate your body so you can receive the nutrients (vitamin D). Inhale and exhale through your nose slowly, inflating your abdomen with each inhale, as you hold this image in your mind for thirty to sixty seconds.

Look Inward *How I feel in my body right now is* . . . Inhale . . . exhale . . .

Giving myself permission to grow now makes me feel . . . Inhale . . . exhale . . .

Receiving the love and encouragement from the energy of the Law of Inspired Action makes me feel . . . Inhale . . . exhale . . .

Emit HUM three to five times.

Activate See it! Visualize the magenta ray in a sunset.

Nourish Feel it! Close your eyes and imagine how this ray of light would touch your heart, body, and mind. Channel this feeling of balance and harmony to the planet through you.

Surrender Say: *I allow confidence. I allow growth. I allow openness. I allow freedom.*

Ease Say: *I am confident. I am open. I am harmony. I am free.*

Cleansing for Empowerment

One of the ways you can recognize the Law of Inspired Action at work is when you see someone following their inner calling. This can show up in a number of ways, from pursuing dreams and desires to standing up for truth and doing what feels right. The Law of Inspired Action can often be illustrated through individuals who are speaking up for themselves, devoted to a cause, or seeking social justice. Again, if it comes from an open inner space (open heart), it is the law. On the other hand, if it is motivated from an inner space of rage, anger, or hatred, this is not the Law of Inspired Action; this is reactivity. It is not that you should quit advocating or caring about certain topics; it is just a sign that you could benefit from a

Cleanse. Once you clear your reactions, you will find that the way you handle things both inside and out changes, and as a result, the things, people, and situations you care about benefit greatly. Martin Luther King Jr. and Rosa Parks are great examples of individuals who were in alignment with this law.

Clear Reactivity   Sit up tall in a comfortable seated position either cross-legged or with your feet flat on the floor. Place your hands, palms up, on your lap. Touch your pointer fingers and thumbs together—creating the "okay" sign with both hands. This is a mudra that represents the universal soul and individual soul as one. Take a few slow deep breaths as you hold this mudra, expanding your lungs and abdomen on each inhale and releasing and contracting your navel to your spine on each exhale.

Look Inward   *How I feel in my body right now is* . . . Inhale . . . exhale . . .

Standing up for my truth makes me feel . . . Inhale . . . exhale . . .

Stepping into my true authentic, divine self now makes me feel . . . Inhale . . . exhale . . .

And when I follow my heart, I feel . . . inhale . . . exhale . . .

Emit   HUM three to five times, extending each one on the exhale.

Activate   See it! Imagine yourself standing tall, head held high, feet flat on the floor. Visualize the magenta ray underneath your feet or behind you.

Nourish   Feel it. Tap in to the brilliance of this ray of light. Allow it to penetrate your image, filtering through you down into Mother Earth. May anyone on this planet who is looking to speak up for themselves and stand up for what feels right (calmly and respectfully) benefit from these vibrations.

Surrender   Say: *I allow truth. I allow empowerment. I allow inspiration. I allow freedom.*

Ease   Say: *I am truth. I am empowerment. I am divinity. I am free.*

MANIFESTING MESSAGE

The Law of Inspired Action shows up in multiple ways. If you are unsure if the reflections of people, situations, or opportunities around you have been inspired by this law, you may also ask the universe, "Please send it to me in another way." Asking the universe for clarification or additional support is another form of taking action. Remember, these laws are based on movement, so their vibrations run at very high levels. They don't come from fear; they come from love. The magenta ray will give you the balance and harmony you need to listen.

Affirmation: The rise and expansion of my own energy inspire me now.

CHAPTER 12

The Law of Perpetual Transmuted Energy

Tune in to this law to . . .
Create something new. Develop your manifesting skills.
Transform energy.

This law reminds us that energy is always in a state of motion and is constantly changing form. Author Wallace D. Wattles states in his book *The Science of Getting Rich*, "The Law of Perpetual Transmutation is energy from the formless realm that is constantly flowing into the material world and taking form."

"Form" can be anything from a thought to an image, feeling, idea, or a tangible (physical) item. This law also reminds us that we are all one big giant sea of consciousness. Our individual thoughts and beliefs are form as well as our collective consciousness. For example, if a large group of people feel oppressed, this takes on a form. While this may seem overwhelming, this law reminds you that you are an individual soul connected to a collective consciousness, and therefore, by transmuting the energy within yourself, you can have a massive impact on others.

Here is one way this law can get misinterpreted: you may feel like the energy inside you is "stuck." For example, you may feel a heaviness in your heart that won't go away even though you took some time to care for yourself. Maybe you went for a walk, meditated, or took some breaths, yet the feeling remains. Just because you don't feel a physical change (for example, lighter in your energy) doesn't mean change is not happening—this is where the Law of Perpetual Transmuted Energy comes into play. You see, sometimes the energy in motion is happening in a higher dimension. In other words, things are changing and shifting; you just haven't experienced it in physical form. If the Law of Perpetual Transmuted Energy could talk, it would say, *Be patient.*

I find it can help to get up and move your body before Cleansing. Sometimes I visualize a ray of light (like yellow, white, or magenta) while lifting my arms overhead (stretching upward), then releasing them down toward the earth (bending into a forward fold), and then rising up again. As I move the energy with my hands, I remember the Law of Perpetual Transmuted Energy says we are always in a state of movement and change. Think about it: Is your hair growing right now? Are the cells in your body changing? The answer is yes; you are never the same moment to moment. The rays of light magnify these internal shifts in powerful ways.

You are disconnected from this law when . . .

- You numb your feelings (perhaps by staying busy or using social media excessively).
- You feel stuck.
- You dislike or overfocus on uncertainty.
- You shut down your feelings (perhaps by blocking or numbing).
- You take things personally or feel easily offended or defensive.
- You feel heavy, constricted, stuck, or bored.
- You are running ahead of yourself, thinking about the sixth thing on your list before tackling the first one.
- You are afraid of your own negative thoughts, and that you may be causing more harm.
- You are wondering what else to do with your life.
- You feel deflated, misled, or confused.

You are connected to this law when . . .

- You take time to process what you feel.
- You pace yourself or let others lead the process.

- You shed old aspects of yourself.
- You feel grounded and calm.
- You sense and feel lightness.
- You trust what you see in your mind's eye.
- You feel open, clear, and secure.
- You see the unknown as a state of possibility.

CORRESPONDING RAY OF LIGHT: RED OR RUBY

The red or ruby ray of light is a wonderful one to work with when you are looking to ground yourself. You are not just grounding to the earth; you are grounding in love. When it comes to transmuting energy (emotions), grounding is key. This is why the first step of Cleansing includes centering tools, ones that direct you to your breath and body. When called upon, the red ray helps you release old resentments and love and accept yourself unconditionally. It also carries vibrations of detachment, transformation, and peace, making it ideal for helping individuals or groups of people who feel oppressed by their situation or addictions.

THE LAW OF PERPETUAL TRANSMUTED ENERGY: COMPANION CLEANSES

Cleansing for Grounding

Rachael wasn't sure why her mother said some of the things she said. While Rachael loved her mother very much, she felt that her mom, at times, could be a little inconsiderate, especially when it came to the way she spoke to Rachael's dad. Although this had been going on for years, Rachael wasn't sure why it bothered her; after all, it was their marriage. After moving through a Cleanse and connecting to the Law of Perpetual Transmuted Energy, Rachael received a new way of viewing her mom. Rather than see her mom as critical, she learned to instead recognize that these comments were a sign her mother was not grounded. As Rachael connected to the red/ruby ray of light during this Cleanse, I encouraged her to filter the light into the space where these dynamics were occurring between her,

her mother, and her father. Right away, Rachael could feel the shift. From that day forward, I encouraged Rachael to call upon the red ray of light any time she recognized her mother (or anyone else for that matter) was losing her sense of being grounded. Our Cleanse looked something like this:

Clear Reactivity With the peace fingers on your dominant hand, press gently about once inch above your navel, with your fingers about three inches apart, for a count of three. Do this three times as you sit up tall. Place your opposite hand (two fingers) on top of your head as you do the gentle presses with the lower hand.

Look Inward *How I feel in my body right now is* . . . Inhale . . . exhale . . .

Releasing this tension from my body now makes me feel . . . Inhale . . . exhale . . .

Connecting to the red ray of light now makes me feel . . . Inhale . . . exhale . . .

Emit HUM three to five times, grounding yourself in unconditional love.

Activate See it! Visualize a ruby-red ray as a flower, sunset, or maybe an ember in a fireplace.

Nourish Feel it! Sense the vibration of this color, and let it flow through the crown of your head, generously down into Mother Earth, grounding in the energy deep in the core.

Surrender Say: *I allow grounding. I allow centering. I allow transmutation. I allow infinite love.*

Ease Say: *I am infinite love. I am calm. I am centered. I am free.*

Cleansing for Well-Being

Have you ever had a time where you felt like you were chasing something? Perhaps you were going after a dream, relationship, success, or a high. While going after the things you desire can be a great motivator, sometimes this inner drive can get a little out of hand.

Perhaps you take on too many projects, work too many hours, or find yourself chasing something that is not good for you—things like partying (a little too much), overeating, overworking, or overspending. You know it because you are having trouble living in the present moment, are distracted by outside influences, or are driven predominately by external rewards. This Cleanse gives you a chance to release some of those tendencies so you can renew your overall well-being. This makes it a whole lot easier for you to connect to the Law of Perpetual Transmuted Energy.

Clear Reactivity   Take a moment now and do what is called lion's breath. Sit up tall, and inhale deeply through your nose, inflating your abdomen. Then on an exhale, open your mouth wide, stick out your tongue, and make the sound HAA. Inhale and repeat this two or three more times.

Look Inward   *How I feel in my body right now is* . . . Inhale . . . exhale . . .

Creating balance and harmony in my life now makes me feel . . . Inhale . . . exhale . . .

Grounding and centering myself in this way now makes me feel . . . Inhale . . . exhale . . .

Emit   HUM three to five times to release overextending.

Activate   See it! Visualize an image of balance, calm, and health, perhaps rocks balancing on a beach. Bring in the red ray.

Nourish   Feel it! Allow the ruby ray to bring healing, balance, and wellness to Mother Earth.

Surrender   Say: *I allow grounding. I allow presence. I allow well-being. I allow love.*

Ease   Say: *I am presence. I am well-being. I am love grounding through love.*

Cleansing for Engagement

One thing I have learned through Cleansing is that there are all sorts of ways people manage their emotions. As you can imagine, some are more positive than others. One of the not-so-great ways is passive-aggressive behavior. This is when someone consciously chooses to do or not do something as a way to spite another person. For example, if someone focuses on their phone even after the other person expresses how it bothers them (particularly during dinner) and they continue to do so, this can come across as harsh or insensitive. As a result, distance may develop between the two individuals; each might feel hurt, annoyed, irritated, or offended. This distancing can cause a numbing of emotions. In other words, each person has to shut down, and the challenge when this occurs is that empathy, love, and trust also become compromised. These are situations where the Law of Perpetual Transmuted Energy can help. It can do this by transmuting isolation, numbness, and disconnection into connection, engagement, and love. The key is not to feed behaviors you don't care for. So if someone is paying more attention to their phone, don't overfocus on their behavior (energy). Instead, move the energy inside yourself and call on the red ray of light for assistance. See it in your mind's eye and imagine showering it throughout your aura and beyond. You are a magical person; don't forget that. Use your spiritual tools rather than your reactivity to transmute the energy.

Clear Reactivity   Imagine placing a cool cloth on your face. Breathe into this cool cloth as a way to wake up your senses. Inhale and exhale through your nose two or three times.

Looking Inward   *How I feel in my body right now is* . . . Inhale . . . exhale . . .

Releasing these patterns of behavior through me now makes me feel . . . Inhale . . . exhale . . .

Transmuting energy in this way now makes me feel . . . Inhale . . . exhale . . .

Emit HUM three to five times as you release and transform.

Activate See it! Imagine an image of engagement, perhaps holding hands, breathing in fresh air, or smelling flowers. Bring in the red ray of light.

Nourish Feel it! Saturate your cells with the red ray. Allow it to transform and transmute any negative or hard feelings into pure love and light. May anyone who is numbing their feelings benefit from this energy as you transport it through you down into Mother Earth.

Surrender Say: *I allow grounding. I allow love. I allow transformation. I allow engagement.*

Ease Say: *I am grounding. I am progressing. I am transformation. I am free.*

Cleansing for Creativity

The Law of Perpetual Transmuted Energy teaches us that we have the ability to both create and uncreate something. In other words, you can manifest both form and formless. Let me give you an example. Let's say a story of feeling rejected or being alone pops into your mind and tuning in to these feelings starts to make you feel tight and constricted inside. Now, I want you to uncreate that story.

Imagine a story of connection, togetherness, and unity. See, you have the ability to create and uncreate things. The Law of Perpetual Transmuted Energy takes this to a bigger scale. It reminds you that when you feel strength on the inside, you produce energy on the outside. Should you have a feeling of insecurity on the inside, you can uncreate it. Energy is always in motion, oscillating between creating and uncreating. By now, I hope you can see how your higher abilities are there; they are just untapped.

You have the power to transform anything. The key is to do it with nonjudgment. As you practice, your ability to produce, create, and manifest gets stronger.

Clear Reactivity   Sit up nice and tall in a comfortable seated position. Relax your face and jaw. With the pads of your fingers on both hands, gently tap your face. Touch it lightly and tap all along your face, waking up the nerve endings in your skin. Be mindful of your eyes. Do this for about twenty seconds, and then take an inhale and exhale (slowly).

Look Inward   *How I feel in my body right now is . . .* Inhale . . . exhale . . .

Now that I understand this law more fully, I feel . . . Inhale . . . exhale . . .

Being connected to my creative powers now makes me feel . . . Inhale . . . exhale . . .

Emit   HUM three to five times.

Activate   Visualize the red ray of light. Tune in to it as a creative force.

Nourish   Receive the red ray of unconditional love, stability, and grounding. Allow it to re-create anything that no longer serves you and the planet.

Surrender   Say: *I allow unconditional love. I allow creation. I allow transmuted energy.*

Ease   Say: *I am unconditional love. I am creation. I am transmuted energy. I am powerful.*

MANIFESTING MESSAGE

You are a multidimensional being. You have many strengths, talents, and abilities. These gifts go far beyond what you can see. You don't have to run everything through your physical body. In other words, you don't have to take on other people's pain in order to understand and transmute it. Remember, the rays of light are alive, conscious frequencies. Let them do the work for you. It is important to remember that the rays of light are not fixing you, as you are already perfect in the eyes of your creator. Instead, they help you to ascend so you can *notice, observe, allow, and receive* your experiences from a higher vibration. It is then that you are able to fully live in accordance with the laws. It is then that you begin to harness your ability to manifest.

Affirmation: Transforming energy comes easily and naturally to me now. Thank you.

CHAPTER 13

The Law of Compensation

Tune in to this law to . . .
Bring in balance. Move into effortlessness.
Elevate abundance.

The Law of Compensation states that you will always be rewarded based on the amount of effort you put in. If you put in quite a bit of effort, you will be compensated for that. If you put in little to no effort, you will likely get back similar to what you gave. Now, I understand that this may not seem right. It may bring to mind a few areas of your life where you feel like you are giving way more than you are receiving.

Keep in mind, the word "compensation" means to pay back or reimburse. Therefore, it makes sense that most people associate this law with money or things. However, we aren't always compensated in that way. Think of individuals who volunteer. They may not get paid in a monetary way per se, but they are likely to tell you the reward comes in different ways. They may be compensated through skill development, special friendships, mentorship, opportunities, or positive vibes.

After working a Cleanse with this law and noticing how people get misaligned and even blocked by it, I noticed a few things. First, the word "effort" tends to trip people up. This is why I suggest you replace "effort" with "energy." The law reads, "You will be compensated according to the quality of *energy* you put in"—this is not just physical and mental energy but emotional energy as well. In other words, if there is fear, judgment, or resentment around what you are creating, that will influence your compensation.

Pay attention to moments where you might be rushing or feel urged to make a decision. Ask, *Am I putting too much pressure on myself?* Pressure and expectations are not effort. Just because you are feeling stressed doesn't equate to effort (or energy) with this law. If anything, the universe may interpret it as noneffort, or even resistance, because of the limited movement pattern of stressful states.

To align with this law, it is important to bring balance into your life by taking the time to connect to the four intentions of *noticing, observing, allowing, and receiving,* even if for only ten minutes a day. This will help you open your energy, making you feel light, open, grounded, and free. The Cleanses and rays of light can help too.

Think of the process of working with the Law of Compensation as a renewal system, a way to replenish yourself. When you relax your energy, quit trying to push your way to the top, and instead let yourself go through the motions, you see how the Law of Compensation is working in your life. Remember, these Spiritual Laws don't sleep. They are always in motion, even when you are asleep.

If you are worrying a lot, you may find yourself attracting other people with a lot of problems. You may think, *Why does everyone tell me about their stuff?* At first, it may seem flattering when someone comes to you for council and shares their personal frustrations, yet over time, you may find you are giving more than you are getting back from such relationships. This may be a sign you are out of alignment with this law.

If you have become used to people putting you down or if being fatigued all the time has become a way of life, then you are out of alignment with this law. You are no longer being renewed. There may be many reasons for this, but the one I most often see is people "normalizing" their situations. They make working endless hours a "normal" way of life, leaving little to no down time, or again, they put too much pressure on themselves, expecting themselves to get from A to Z in just a short while. Take it easy. Renew, serve, contribute to the planet, and align with those four intentions. Remember, life is not a race. Move through the Cleanses below so you can notice the ways you are being guided and compensated for the quality of energy you put in.

You are disconnected from this law when . . .

○ You spend more money than you make.
○ You put a lot of pressure on yourself.
○ You see other people's success as a reflection of what you are not.
○ You worry about the future.
○ You feel trapped, stuck, or limited by your resources or situation.
○ You find you are a magnet for people telling you their problems (unsolicited).
○ You are being cheap (not just with money, but also in offering praise and encouragement).
○ You feel jealous or envious of other people's success.
○ You are normalizing behaviors and ways of life (like doing all the work with no support).
○ You say things like, "I don't have enough work," or "We don't have enough money."

You are connected to this law when . . .

○ You have a voice, you trust, and you have faith.
○ You are using your intuition as a source of guidance.
○ You notice blessings or moments of gratitude.
○ You can see some peaceful options and choices.
○ You see multiple avenues and opportunities.
○ You are not taking things personally (you may even have compassion).
○ You are able to receive feedback in a constructive (rather than a self-critical) way.
○ You offer praise and encouragement to others.
○ You are willing to forgive.
○ You are having new experiences, thoughts, feelings, and awareness.

○ You are open and interested in new conversations and topics, like education, history, or healing.

○ You are able to reframe mistakes as learning.

CORRESPONDING RAY OF LIGHT: GREEN

The green ray of light carries vibrations of healing, balance, abundance, and miracles. It offers the energy of truth. The green ray is a perfect companion for the Law of Compensation (and renewal) as it provides deep healing for your conscious mind, subconscious, and soul. The green ray brings a sense of comfort by reminding you that you have the capacity to heal and transform old wounds. If you feel broken or are carrying a scarcity (not-enough) belief system, the green ray will give you just the amount of nourishment you need to feel whole again. You are perfect in the eyes of your creator.

THE LAW OF COMPENSATION:
COMPANION CLEANSES

Cleansing for Discernment

Priscilla could not decide between two dentists. One had great reviews yet charged three times as much money, while the other one charged less but had mediocre reviews. Since the procedure she needed was not covered by insurance, you can imagine this was a difficult decision. The reality was that Priscilla didn't really trust either dentist. No matter who she picked, she felt like she was on the losing end.

Tapping into the green ray of light helped Priscilla let go and trust. At first, she found herself resisting the ray (by turning to negative thinking), yet through the intentions of *noticing, observing, allowing, and receiving,* she eventually gave herself permission to trust the process. I find this is common; most people are not accustomed to handling things in this way. Archangel Raphael is one of many who oversee this ray. It is all connected to source (the God of your understanding).

Eventually Priscilla was able to make her decision, and later she told me she visualized the green light around her during the procedure.

You may do that as well: imagine the green ray (outside of the Cleanse) anytime you are looking for healing, balance, or support.

Clear Reactivity   Roll your shoulders up, back, and down a few times. Then dip your right ear toward your right shoulder, pause, and hold for about three seconds. Bring your head back to center, receive your in-breath, and then tilt your left ear toward your left shoulder for three seconds. Bring your head back to center, take an inhale, and exhale.

Look Inward   *How I feel in my body right now is* . . . Inhale . . . exhale . . .

Now that I know how to take care of my own energy, I feel . . . Inhale . . . exhale . . .

Being compensated in this way now makes me feel . . . Inhale . . . exhale . . .

Emit   HUM three to five times.

Activate   See it! Visualize the green ray of light. Which hue of the green ray comes to mind? It can be anything from emerald green to light green. Just notice.

Nourish   Feel it! Filter the green ray of light into the situation and into your field of energy. Imagine how the vibrations of abundance, truth, and balance would feel on your skin. How might that relax and comfort you? Receive these rays on a greater scale. Soak up the green ray of light for the world.

Surrender   Say: *I allow abundance. I allow healing. I allow discernment. I allow freedom.*

Ease   Say: *I am healing. I am abundance. I am discernment. I am free.*

Cleansing for Abundance

Take a moment right now and ask yourself what "abundant" means to you. If you could see an image of abundance, what would it look like? Flowing water, fields of green, cars, money, vacations? Let's be honest, what would you see? To be abundant means to have very large quantities. Since our emotions are abstract, we don't really think of them as a resource of abundance, yet they are (when they are in flow). Listen, I know there are a lot of people who could use help right now, and sometimes it feels selfish or wrong to think about abundance in this way, yet you are not hurting anyone by imaging these things, are you? The point is, it is okay to imagine and dream as long as it doesn't come from ego (which results in a false sense of security and power).

Energy in motion is abundance; energy in action is abundance. What follows this energy and the things you attract, do, and see are not up to you; they are up to your creator. Your job is to cultivate the energy in action and let the universe do the rest. You can't ask for abundance and restrict it at the same time. The Law of Compensation doesn't work that way.

Abundance isn't *a thing*; it is a feeling, a well of sensations. These sensations provide internal shifts. If you are not sure whether you can handle the energy, be assured the Cleanse structure will anchor you. Some of these internal shifts are experienced as changes in temperature, for example, from warm to cool. While some people might feel a tightness come in followed by a calming release, others report a tingly sensation on their limbs.

When the Law of Compensation is working, you will know it because opportunities come to you with more ease. Then your job as a creator is to choose the one that feels right.

Clear Reactivity Sit up tall. With your dominant hand, press those three acupressure points above your navel—one inch above the navel with the fingers one inch apart. With your other hand, press your forehead (gently) with two fingers. Hold your fingers on your forehead as you use your lower hand to press for a count of three. Release your hands to your lap.

Look Inward *How I feel in my body right now is. . .* Inhale . . . exhale . . .

Sitting in the HUM vibration now makes me feel . . . Inhale . . . exhale . . .

When I tune in to the energy of abundance, I feel . . . Inhale . . . exhale . . .

Emit   HUM three to five times, releasing any restriction.

Activate   See it! Visualize a big tree with hundreds of branches, vast fields, or the smell of fresh-cut grass. Or just picture the green ray of light in your mind.

Nourish   Feel it! Nourish yourself with its healing rays. Allow anyone on the planet who may benefit from more abundance in their life to receive the benefits of this Cleanse.

Surrender   Say: *I allow abundance. I allow healing. I allow truth. I allow miracles.*

Ease   Say: *I am abundance. I am miracles. I am truth. I am energy. I am free.*

Cleansing for Acceptance

Before beginning this Cleanse, take a moment to reflect on the energy of denial. To deny means to withhold, ignore, or withdraw. For example, you may have a feeling of distrust. Perhaps you wonder if a friend or loved one is doing something behind your back. Rather than have an open, honest discussion with that person, instead you deny the feeling of suspicion, hurt, or fear. Yet as you know, those feelings don't necessarily disappear, and therefore, to keep them at bay, you may develop denial systems, thoughts, and behaviors that keep these emotions at a distance. For example, you may withdraw love and affection from this person. Perhaps you tell yourself you are not going to call or text them anymore.

While this might provide some distance, take a moment and think about the energy of denial (like withdrawal). Inevitably, you send a message to the universe that you are withdrawing (rather than depositing, growing, creating) energy. Over time, this will contribute to states of depletion and, as I like to call it, spiritual dehydration. You can see how this might influence your relationship with the Law of Compensation. Think in terms of deposits, my friend. What energy are you depositing (producing, generating, moving) today? Choose to deposit the green ray.

Clear Reactivity   Sit up tall in a comfortable seated position. With your fingers, massage your scalp for about twenty seconds in a way that feels right to you. You can either dig in, scrubbing really fast (like you are washing your hair), or, using the pads of your fingers, massage softly and slowly. After twenty seconds, move to the next step.

Look Inward   *How I feel in my body right now is* . . . Inhale . . . exhale . . .

Now that I am conscious about the energy I am producing, I feel . . . Inhale . . . exhale . . .

Receiving these deposits of truth and abundance now makes me feel . . . Inhale . . . exhale . . .

Emit   HUM three to five times as you release and transform your denial systems, like worry, control, or fear.

Activate   See it! Visualize the green ray of light generously expanding inside and around you.

Nourish   Feel it! Receive this ray, allowing it to lift the energy of denial and transforming it into truth, healing, and abundance for all.

Surrender   Say: *I allow healing. I allow abundance. I allow prosperity. I allow energy.*

Ease   Say: *I am depositing. I am growing. I am thriving. I am renewal. I am free.*

Cleansing for Gratitude

Over the years, I have worked with many individuals who found themselves in unhealthy and, at times, abusive relationships. While I knew gratitude could be a powerful force for helping them to regain their spirit, I knew it needed to happen on their own time and in their own way. While it may seem impossible to be grateful for something so hurtful and destructive, it is not about being grateful for what happened, but rather it's an opportunity to release a deep-seated pattern. Sometimes these patterns of reactivity (emotional suppression) are so well hidden that without a Cleanse, it could take years to uncover them.

There are many blessings in your life. I am sure you know that on some level. Just the fact that you are alive on this planet is a miracle. While the experience of gratitude (similar to happiness) can come and go, tapping into the green ray of light can help distribute gratitude here on the planet. As this occurs, you won't need a reason to be grateful; you just will be. A simple thank-you to the universe will do. Imagine waking up in pure gratitude every day. Imagine no longer having the need to identify or acknowledge it because it just is. Trust; even if you don't, your spirit does.

Clear Reactivity   Sit up tall and rub your hands together vigorously for about twenty seconds. Separate your hands and place them on the sides of your cheeks. Hold your face in your hands for about twenty seconds while closing your eyes and breathing in and out through your nose. Release your hands and move to the next step.

Look Inward   *How I feel in my body right now is* . . . Inhale . . . exhale . . .

Having this breakthrough now makes me feel . . . Inhale . . . exhale . . .

Creating space for love and gratitude in my life now makes me feel . . . Inhale . . . exhale . . .

Emit   HUM five long times. Inhale through your nose and exhale as you release blocked, constricted energy and the reaction of normalizing.

Activate   See it! Visualize an image of motion and opening, perhaps a field of green or a stream of moving water. Or picture the green ray of light around you now.

Nourish   Feel it! Sense the healing, cleansing, and nourishing vibrations of the green ray. Relax your body when it is present. This will allow you to take in more of this beautiful light.

Surrender   Say: *I allow abundance. I allow breakthroughs. I allow love. I allow freedom.*

Ease   Say: *I am abundance. I am energy. I am light. I am free.*

MANIFESTING MESSAGE

Throughout your life, you will be compensated in many ways. It is important for you to keep your energy fresh, vibrant, and flowing so you are able to really take in these opportunities when they occur. This allows you to feel full, not like the full after eating a large meal. This is more of an inner fulfillment, the kind that makes you feel lighter, connected, more peaceful, and freer. This is what true abundance is. It is about feeling so full that you are able to release easily and effortlessly, knowing you are already in a state of abundance. Each time you release, you create space to receive.

Affirmation: I am open and willing to receive.

CHAPTER 14

The Law of Relativity

Tune in to this law to . . .
Become more neutral. Decrease attachment to meaning.
Be in the here and now.

The Law of Relativity teaches us that everything in our life simply *is* until we compare it to something. Nothing in life has any meaning, except for the meaning we give it. Up until that point of reaction, everything is neutral. In other words, the situations, people, and things you may be looking at did not take on the meaning you gave them until you compared your circumstances to something else. For example, you may imagine what your life would look like before or after going through a difficult time. For example, if you are in the process of getting a divorce, you may be comparing married life to single life in both positive and negative ways. If you are entering retirement, you may compare a busy life to a boring life. People do this all the time; they talk about what life was like before they had children, gained weight, changed their careers, or gained or lost money.

While reflecting on your life isn't necessarily a bad thing, if the meanings and interpretations you place on these events are disrupting your sense of inner peace, you may begin to see evidence of it in your outer world. Sometimes these disruptions show up in our sleep patterns, anxiety levels, and relationships. For example, let's imagine your workplace is going through a lot of changes, and as a result, there is uncertainty and stress in the air. According to the Law of Relativity, you only see things as worse, bad, or toxic because you are comparing them to what you knew or how you fantasized things would be before you were in the situation. If the Law of Relativity could speak, it would say, *Soften, relax, and allow things to rearrange themselves.* When things are in the middle of transforming (and sometimes that looks like things are upside-down and sideways), pull out this mantra: *My presence is enough.*

Choose to cultivate the four intentions: *notice, observe, allow, and receive.* Call upon a ray of light.

You are disconnected from this law when . . .

○ You feel out of control, perhaps experiencing mood changes or high levels of distractibility.
○ You go to your head (thoughts) to interpret what you feel (sensation wise) rather than your higher self.
○ You revisit the same emotions (perhaps anger, frustration, rage) over and over.
○ You feel like giving up.
○ You engage in obsessive-compulsive behavior (and may be getting negative attention for it).
○ You are ruminating or analyzing your situation.
○ You feel like you don't have a choice.

You are connected to this law when . . .

○ You sense the energy in and around you without judgment.
○ You can approach yourself and others gently and with compassion.
○ You can see situations and events as part of your spiritual journey.
○ You recognize your choices and lead from your heart.
○ You are able to listen, understand, and tend to your bodily and emotional needs.
○ You ask your higher self, guides, and the universe to give you more information about what you feel inside (rather than relying only on your mind).

CORRESPONDING RAY OF LIGHT: SILVER

The silver ray of light is the counterpart to the gold ray. It holds high universal energy. Initially, this ray may seem gray, and as you open yourself up to it, notice if it gains a shimmery, silver appearance. The silver ray carries aspects of divine mother consciousness. Therefore, it is a very nurturing ray, awakening the divine feminine in you and bringing balance to perhaps the strong masculine (dominant, assertive) energies around you.

THE LAW OF RELATIVITY: COMPANION CLEANSES

Cleansing for Effectiveness

When emotional energy gets high or intense, without a healthy outlet, it can lead to self-destructive behavior. For example, I have seen people who started with a little crush on someone, and then it led to an obsession. With social media, that can be so easy to do these days—watching every move someone makes. Yet, when something gets to a level in which it consumes you, you are probably giving a ton of attention and energy to it. It is like filling your tank with gas and then driving around all day instead of actually attending to the things that are most important (and give you energy)—like your health, exercise, current relationships, talents, and hobbies. While in the moment, it might be kind of fun and exciting to binge on sugar or have sex with someone you hardly know, but after a while, you may find yourself frustrated with where you are in your life. You know this is the case when you start thinking, dwelling, or believing the stories in your head that tell you that you are not good enough.

Clear Reactivity   Sit up tall and relax your shoulders and your diaphragm. Take a nice slow inhale, and on the exhale, make an audible sound through your mouth, such as AHH, LAA, or VAM. Repeat two or three times.

Look Inward   *How I feel in my body right now is* . . . Inhale . . . exhale . . .

Using my energy efficiently now makes me feel . . . Inhale . . . exhale . . .

Bringing myself back to this present moment to fully experience what is now makes me feel . . . Inhale . . . exhale . . .

Emit   HUM three to five times, releasing and transforming pent-up energy.

Activate   See it! Visualize the silver ray of light. Watch it glisten, similar to the way moonlight bounces off water.

Nourish   Feel it! Receive the frequencies of the silver ray. Allow it to nurture you with unconditional love, balance, and security. May all beings who share a similar pattern receive this awakening.

Surrender   Say: *I allow gentleness. I allow effectiveness. I allow good fortune. I allow freedom.*

Ease   Say: *I am fortunate. I am valuable. I am harmless, gentle. I am free.*

Cleansing for Courage

Have you ever had a time when you did not feel included? Or perhaps you felt like you could not trust the people around you. Maybe you felt like they were talking behind your back or purposely treating you like you were annoying or a pain in the butt. Perhaps, in some ways, you see yourself as a victim. In those moments, you may feel alone and unprotected, and if you sit in the energy long enough, you may find yourself pushing through heavy energy. If so, you are not alone. These kinds of reactive patterns are far too common.

Tuning in to the silver ray can give you the strength and courage you need to transform any beliefs you developed during those periods of your life. Allow the ray to neutralize all those experiences from a kind and loving space. As you develop this inner space, courage will begin to come. I promise. Anyone can get up and fight, but it takes courage to stand up for what you believe and need without retaliation. I always say, sometimes the most courageous thing you can do is choose to feel. It is the moment when your vibration is crossing the threshold (energy in action) of fear into love.

Clear Reactivity   Rub your hands together vigorously for twenty seconds. Place one hand on your forehead and the other on the back of your neck. Breathe in and out through your nose, inflating your abdomen on each inhale, for twenty seconds.

Look Inward   *How I feel in my body right now is . . .* Inhale . . . exhale . . .

Neutralizing beliefs and interpretations about myself makes me feel . . . Inhale . . . exhale . . .

Having the courage to let love in now makes me feel . . . Inhale . . . exhale . . .

Emit   HUM three to five times.

Activate   See it! Visualize an image of courage, perhaps a mountaintop or a peaceful warrior. Or imagine the silver ray of light.

Nourish   Feel it! Pour the ray of silver light through your image. Disperse it freely to all living beings.

Surrender   Say: *I allow strength. I allow leadership. I allow healing. I allow freedom.*

Ease   Say: *I am strong. I am focused. I am courageous. I am clear. I am free.*

Cleansing for Focus

The moment you compare yourself or your situation to something else, you have lost your focus. You took your eye off the ball and got distracted by your thoughts. While you can't stop yourself from thinking, you can interrupt the flow, frequency, and rate that thoughts occur.

I like to describe triggered thoughts like auto-subscriptions. You know those annoying emails that send you coupons and notifications? If you are like me, you might be inclined to unsubscribe from them. When you do, have you ever noticed a little box pops up to ask you, *Are you sure?* This is where the Law of Relativity can help. Unsubscribing felt right, until you compared it to something else, right? It is all relative. In other words, don't give something so small (like unsubscribing from an email list) so much energy. Don't make a mountain out of a molehill. Let it go, and should it be meant to be in your life, you can bet the universe will send it back.

Let's cleanse.

Clear Reactivity   Sit up tall and rub your hands vigorously together for twenty seconds while breathing in and out through your nose. After twenty seconds, place one of your hands on the back of your neck (palm down). Breathe in and out through your nose for one inhale and one exhale. Then do the same with the other hand, breathing in and out through your nose one time.

Look Inward   *How I feel in my body right now is* . . . Inhale . . . exhale . . .

And when I let things go, I feel . . . Inhale . . . exhale . . .

Letting things be as they are makes me feel . . . Inhale . . . exhale . . .

Being focused and present to what is happening right now makes me feel . . . Inhale . . . exhale . . .

Emit   HUM three to five times, releasing triggered thoughts.

Activate   See it! Visualize the silver ray of light coming in and melting all reactivity, similar to the way icicles dissolve in the sun.

Nourish   Feel it! Pour a ray of silver light in the atmosphere. Allow the sparkly rays of this silver light to comfort you, Mother Earth, and anyone else on the planet who may be experiencing auto-thoughts.

Surrender   Say: *I allow release. I allow letting go. I allow space. I allow freedom.*

Ease   Say: *I am liberated. I am truth. I am focus. I am clear. I am free.*

Cleansing for Connection

Weight loss, physical appearance, and self-image consume the lives of so many. Perhaps that's why there are multimillion-dollar industries that "fix" these things. While I am definitely not a nutritionist, I have met many people (including myself) who are frustrated with trying to maintain a certain weight or image. Using the example of craving sugar, here is how the Law of Relativity can help.

From the law's point of view, the reason you experience sugar as one thing and vegetables as another is because you compare them, right? You use your brain and sensory system—senses of taste, smell, and texture—to help you make these comparisons. Your brain helps you remember or associate certain foods with certain things or experiences. The Spiritual Laws remind you that you are not your brain or the associated memories. You are a spirit first. In other words, if you take away your brain, everything is just energy. It just is. Your experience is a reflection of the relationship you are having with energy in that moment.

When you get overinvolved in comparing and contrasting (for example this person is fat, this person is thin, this person is healthy, this person is a hot mess), you disconnect from this law. It is all relative. Your brain and body provide the means for you to have this experience in a physical body. Your experience in a physical body is determined by your sensory system (your senses of smell, taste, texture, temperature), and by the way, this includes your ability to sense energy. The four intentions help you navigate your sensory system and move energy. In other words, *notice, observe, allow, and receive.* Connect to both what you can see and what you cannot see (energy).

This is where it all comes together. The challenge is that some of the chemicals in our foods confuse our sensory and nervous systems. They have been modified so greatly that they literally mess with people's guts. Yet, at the purest rawest form, everything is energy, and everything is relative. The Law of Relativity reminds you that you only think you are fat, chubby, or whatever, because you have that comparison. If you strip it all away, you'll see that it is all energy moving at different frequencies. Start living your life as a spiritual being, get to know energy in its rawest, purest form, and make everything about energy rather than an outcome.

Clear Reactivity Sit up tall in a comfortable seated position. Place one hand on your heart and the other on your abdominal area. As you hold your heart steady with your hand, breathe into your lower abdomen area, inflating it on the inhale for a count of four, and then deflate, pulling your navel toward your spine for a count of four. Do this a couple of times in a row.

Look Inward *How I feel in my body right now is* . . . Inhale . . . exhale . . .

And when I treat everything as energy, I feel . . . Inhale . . . exhale . . .

Detaching from comparisons now makes me feel . . . Inhale . . . exhale . . .

Now that I am choosing to honor and be present to what is, I feel . . . Inhale . . . exhale . . .

Emit HUM three to five times to release disconnection.

Activate See it! Visualize connection, perhaps groups of people working in a garden together gathering food for all. Or just imagine the silver ray of light.

Nourish Feel it! Download the silver ray of light into your cells, heart, and body. Allow it to filter through you into Mother Earth, enhancing the vibration of connection onto the planet now.

Surrender Say: *I allow nourishment. I allow love. I allow connection. I allow freedom.*

Ease Say: *I am connected. I am love. I am fulfilled. I am free.*

MANIFESTING MESSAGE

If you have a habit of comparing yourself to others, then your goal would be to build self-esteem and confidence. The intention that will fuel this goal is to *notice, observe, allow, and receive* inner strength. This means to nourish and support self-love and self-compassion. Notice any areas of your life where you are putting unnecessary pressure on yourself. Tune in to the silver ray of light that has already been activated within you through the previous cleanses. Allow the silver ray to soothe you with love, compassion, and comfort. Sense the silver ray filter through and moving out about twelve inches into your aura. Take an inhale and exhale as you imagine this ray.

Affirmation: I am growing, expanding, and creating new pathways every day.

CHAPTER 15

The Law of Polarity

Tune in to this law . . .
To increase acceptance. For Protection. For forgiveness.

The Law of Polarity teaches us that everything has an opposite; everything has a pole. For example, love and hate, masculine energy and feminine energy, yin and yang. There is always another side of the coin. This tells us we always have a choice. You can either acknowledge (process) or repress what you feel. When it comes to the Cleanse, I often find people's reactions are the exact opposite of what they are looking to create. In other words, they may want more peace in their lives but choose to worry or ruminate.

You might witness the Law of Polarity in your life through relationships. Maybe you are close with individuals who are your opposite. For example, you may be an early bird, while your loved one is a night owl. It is not bad or wrong to be different; it just is. Having opposite or opposing energy is not the problem; it is when we judge (rather than honor) these differences that we can run into hardship, disharmony, and pain. Very often reducing judgment and increasing empathy can be enough to bring balance and harmony among each other. If the Law of Polarity could talk, it would say, *Allow differences; they will always exist.* The Law of Polarity shows how moving in the opposite direction (like from reactive to compassionate) is sometimes the best approach you can take.

You are disconnected from this law when . . .

○ You fight with your experiences, people, and situations.

- You shut down your energy or emotions by overemphasizing differences, perhaps through exaggerated complaints or extreme reactions.
- You resist energy, movement, or change.
- You feel a loss of purpose, drained, or numb.
- You feel like you are repeating the same patterns.
- You judge or label others, perhaps calling someone toxic or controlling.

You are connected to this law when . . .

- You accept things, people, and circumstances as they are without trying to change (or judge) them.
- You choose to bring balance and harmony into your life (perhaps taking time to recharge).
- You feel centered and balanced.
- You no longer judge, analyze, or give too much meaning (interpretation) to what someone else is doing.
- You are able to respect and honor differences.
- You choose an opposite reaction.

CORRESPONDING RAY OF LIGHT: INDIGO

The indigo ray carries the vibrations of trust, faith, unity, and surrender. I have seen this ray come through to help people release and purify old ways of seeing things and even physical experiences. For example, one person connected to this ray and immediately got an impression (image) of their liver and fire. Fire is a metaphysical sign for cleansing, and the liver is an organ that cleanses your blood. This was a very powerful message, as this person was looking to manifest healthy cells and organs. Keep in mind you don't have to "see" anything to know transformation is happening; your intention to connect and be open to the rays is enough. When working with this ray, allow it to expand several feet into your aura.

THE LAW OF POLARITY: COMPANION CLEANSES

Cleansing for Forgiveness

Rob grew up in a family where teasing was how they showed each other love and affection. Yet sometimes the teasing went too far, and what started as poking fun ended up in hard feelings. When Rob was younger, he went along with the teasing although inside it made him feel confused and uneasy. Now as an adult, Rob looked back at his upbringing as an unhealthy illustration of the way his family dealt with stress and pain. This made it difficult for him to want to be around his family, particularly when they behaved in similar ways.

Cleansing gave Rob an opportunity to recognize the Law of Polarity at work. Rob saw how his family's form of affection was so different from his. He was able to see how it was their version of affection. Rob desired the opposite. He wanted to feel connected, supported, and loved.

As Rob got to know this law, he started to accept these differences. In other words, he was able to take things less personally. Rather than overfocusing on anger and upset, he did the opposite and allowed these intense feelings to dissolve into vibrations of peace and love. Moving things in this way emotionally (via the Cleanse) allowed Rob to value the opposite, to use it as a reference point of how he wanted to be rather than a review of his past. You may also find it helpful to think of the opposite when you are having intense emotions, such as fear or anger. Rather than focus on the cause, focus on the opposite, on the direction of inner movement you would like. Keep in mind what you are truly heading for is back to source (pure unconditional love).

Clear Reactivity Sit in a comfortable position, with your spine nice and long and chin parallel to the earth. With your right hand, close your right nostril so you breathe exclusively through the left nostril (this induces the relaxation response). Breathe in and out slowly (inflating your abdomen on the inhale) for two or three breaths (deflating your abdomen on the exhale).

Look Inward *How I feel in my body right now is* . . . Inhale . . . exhale . . .

Now that I have this frame of reference, I feel . . . Inhale . . . exhale . . .

Emit *Making new choices makes me feel* . . . Inhale . . . exhale . . .

HUM three to five times, releasing the reactions around what you're forgiving.

Activate See the opposite of what you feel. Rob saw himself releasing a large weight off his shoulders. Or imagine the indigo ray of light, which can appear as dark purple or blue.

Nourish Feel it! Receive the healing rays of the purple light. Receive the vibrations of detachment and peace. This is forgiveness. Put your attention on Mother Earth as you do this.

Surrender Say: *I allow calm. I allow detachment. I allow light. I allow freedom.*

Ease Say: *I am calm. I am detachment. I am light. I am carefree.*

Cleansing for Letting Go

The indigo ray is a wonderful one to work with if you hear yourself repeating certain words, phrases, or opinions. This is because the indigo ray moves any energy in your throat chakra. Before beginning this Cleanse, ask yourself: *What am I holding on to?* Are you holding on to what you want or what you have? What is keeping you from letting go? Notice how the act of holding on is the opposite of letting go.

These are interesting questions to ask yourself when you are working with the Law of Polarity. The point is to recognize how you may be resisting the laws of nature. In other words, differences and opposing forces will always exist. The funny part is, the more you understand and learn to accept this as truth, the easier it will be to move into states of peace and harmony.

For example, notice if there is a belief. Perhaps you believe you are stuck. This law reminds you that this is always an opposite energy. It could be unstuck, liberated, or free. If the Law of

Polarity could talk, it would say, *Let your feelings (not your thoughts) guide you to the opposite. It will happen naturally with movement.* Consider writing down a few feeling words that are resurfacing for you, perhaps words like "doubt," "fear," or "uncertainty." Move through the Cleanse below (to create inner movement) and then write down the opposite of what you are unintentionally creating (through those resurfacing feeling words), perhaps "confidence, faith, and clarity."

Clear Reactivity   Sit up tall in a comfortable seated position. Inhale slowly through your nose (inflating your abdomen) for the count of three and then exhale through your mouth for the count of four, pulling your navel toward your spine. Your exhale is one count longer than your inhale. This will help you connect more deeply to your body. After a few breaths, move to the next step.

Look Inward   *How I feel in my body right now is* . . . Inhale . . . exhale . . .

Now that I have a better understanding of this law, I feel . . . Inhale . . . exhale . . .

Allowing my inner movement to guide me in a new direction now makes me feel . . . Inhale . . . exhale . . .

Emit   HUM three to five times while releasing the need to control.

Activate   See it! Imagine the indigo ray of light. See it filtering its light into the dynamics of your situation.

Nourish   Feel it! Allow the indigo ray to transform reactions for you, leaving you with an overall sense of cleansing and grounding to Mother Earth.

Surrender   Say: *I allow letting go. I allow surrender. I allow acceptance. I allow freedom.*

Ease   Say: *I am letting go. I am validation. I am acceptance. I am free.*

Cleansing for Completion

Have you ever noticed that sometimes things have to go full circle in order for you to feel a sense of completion? In other words, has there ever been a time when you left yourself only to return to yourself? Perhaps you followed someone else's dreams, advice, or suggestions. Maybe you were persuaded to attend medical school only to discover your heart really lies with being a teacher. The Law of Polarity shows you there is always an opposite of who you are, and at times, you may head in that direction. While you may or may not have some regrets about that, know that it may have been exactly what you needed to do to fully appreciate (and be content with) who you are.

If you have ever heard the phrase "the grass isn't always greener on the other side of the fence," you're acquainted with this law. Very often when manifesting, we can get caught up in the "greener" side only to realize that everything we always truly wanted (like the ability to be ourselves) was always inside of us. Yet sometimes you have to go out (in the opposite direction) and test the waters to come to an inner place of peace and freedom.

Clear Reactivity Sit up tall in a comfortable seated position. With the peace fingers of your dominant hand, lightly tap the edge of your left hand. You will tap on what is called the "karate chop" point, which is between the base of your pinkie and wrist. Tap lightly for about thirty seconds as you inhale and exhale through your nose.

Look Inward *How I feel in my body right now is* . . . Inhale . . . exhale . . .

Now that I have a larger perspective, I feel . . . Inhale . . . exhale . . .

Discovering myself makes me feel . . . Inhale . . . exhale . . .

Trusting the universe's plan for me now makes me feel . . . Inhale . . . exhale . . .

Emit HUM three to five times.

Activate   See it! Visualize the indigo ray of light or a circle to signify completion. Or imagine the indigo ray shining through a full moon.

Nourish   Feel it! Nourish yourself with the indigo ray of light. Allow it to shower you with vibrations of faith and freedom.

Surrender   Say: *I allow transformation. I allow compassion. I allow completion. I allow freedom.*

Ease   Say: *I am transformation. I am compassion. I am completion. I am free.*

Cleansing for Protection

In the psychology world, there is something called projection. This is when someone may project their reactions onto you. For example, let's say one of your friends gives you a little bit of a cold shoulder, or maybe they are acting as if they like another friend better. Let's imagine you ask this person if they are upset with you, and they tell you, "No, everything is fine." Yet inside, you notice you feel hurt by what is happening.

There may be a lot of reasons why this could be happening, and projection could be one of them. When someone projects, this is how they react to (rather than process) what they feel. In other words, rather than tell you their true feelings (which they may not be able to identify themselves), they act differently toward you. As you can imagine, this can be very confusing. With the Law of Polarity, sometimes you will witness others behaving the opposite way of what you know, and this can take a toll on your system. You thought you knew or understood this person, yet they feel different. This may scare you or even upset you. This is where the indigo ray of light can help. It moves things along more quickly, transforming any negativity into positive growth. Take a deep breath and go easy on yourself as you never know when the Law of Polarity is in the works. The laws are always at play, interfacing differently with one another. When you think about it, there is so much you don't control. You do however have a say, and your interactions matter, so whatever you choose, do it from a place of awareness and let the rays of light do the rest.

Clear Reactivity Sit up tall in a comfortable seated position. Roll your shoulders back and down a few times to release your neck. With the peace fingers on your dominate hand, gently tap the outer edge of your opposite hand at the karate-chop point (the space between the base of your pinkie and wrist). Inhale and exhale through your nose as you gently tap this area for about thirty seconds.

Look Inward *How I feel in my body right now is* . . . Inhale . . . exhale . . .

Allowing others to do what feels right for them makes me feel . . . Inhale . . . exhale . . .

Taking in the indigo ray now makes me feel . . . Inhale . . . exhale . . .

Emit HUM three to five times, releasing any tendency to internalize projections.

Activate See it! Visualize protection, perhaps the strength of the indigo ray.

Nourish Feel it! Receive the protective and transformative qualities of this ray and allow Mother Earth to receive it as well so all beings can feel safe, happy, and free.

Surrender Say: *I allow divine protection. I allow release. I allow clarity. I allow freedom.*

Ease Say: *I am clarity. I am divine protection. I am worthy. I am free.*

MANIFESTING MESSAGE

When you are too attached to the physical, perhaps how others act or think, you are likely out of sync with this law. For example, if you see discord, arguing, or disagreements around you, it is likely there is too much emphasis on the physical. In other words, you forget the opposite of physical is non-physical. Get to know yourself as a non-physical being of light. The rays of light will help. Conflict requires healing, and healing cannot happen without the intention of love, compassion, forgiveness, and acceptance. These are non-physical states. As you download these rays of light into both your physical and non-physical energy body, be sure to disperse the color throughout your aura (several feet around you) and beyond. If you sense heaviness around you, try stating these words out loud: "I call upon the indigo ray of light." You may even use a sing-song tone when calling in the rays. *Notice, observe, allow, and receive* this experience. You are it!

Affirmation: I am open and enriched by new ways of seeing and experiencing things.

CHAPTER 16

The Law of Giving and Receiving

Tune in to this law to . . .
Offer and allow. Live in harmony. Give freely.

This law is about constant flow and effortless exchange. It is the constant exchange of giving and receiving that keeps the energy of abundance in flow. This law reminds you that when you give, you are contributing to this abundance, and when you receive, you are allowing yourself to have an experience. To experience something fully requires opening and relaxing your energy field—flow. Neither giving nor receiving is better than the other. We need both to live in harmony and circulate abundance.

The Law of Giving and Receiving says that when you give, expect nothing in return, and when you receive, take it in fully; don't deny or restrict the energy. Accept everything as perfect. Know this law is not just about money. It works in accordance with any form of giving and receiving. For example, you may give your time, love, or attention to another. It can be as simple as offering someone a hand, compliment, or smile. Same goes for when you receive. If someone takes time with you, fully receive it. In other words, don't spend half of that time looking at your phone (scrolling through social media); instead, be fully present to the love the person you are with has for you. Be sure not to judge or criticize someone else's efforts.

If you truly want abundance, work with this law. It is right there, always in the works. If you carry the belief that you are alone and unlovable or that you have to do everything (with little support from others), you are out of alignment. Begin to balance yourself out. You may be overdoing it in one of these areas. When you do, the energy of creating the remarkable gets shut down. Stay true to your intentions; the following Cleanses along with the violet ray of light will help.

You are disconnected from this law when . . .

○ You go along with something just so you don't appear needy or like a poor sport.
○ You are longing for affection.
○ You minimize compliments or opportunities to connect with others.
○ You overcompensate for others. For example, you do extra because you believe others aren't capable or won't do their part.
○ You say things like, "I will figure it out," or "It is not a big deal."
○ You take more than you give.
○ You take little to no time for yourself.

You are connected to this law when . . .

○ You practice self-compassion.
○ You say thank you to the universe regardless of what the attraction is.
○ You have discernment. For example, you notice the difference between giving and enabling.
○ You notice what your body feels like when it is deprived of energy (tight, tense) and choose to receive more (via the intentions).
○ You give without expecting anything in return.
○ You are genuinely happy for others.

- You are able to say thank you to your attractions (even if they were uncomfortable).
- You feel a sense of inner fulfillment.
- You enjoy both giving and receiving.

CORRESPONDING RAY OF LIGHT: VIOLET

The violet ray is often referred to as the ray of transformation. It is capable of giving you a third-eye activation, opening up your psychic and higher awareness abilities. The violet ray is powerful. Not only does it transmute energy (emotions), but it also carries the qualities of abundance, justice, freedom, and mercy. It fosters forgiveness and justice while promoting alchemy.

The violet ray is often referred to as the seventh ray. In situations where trust needs to be rebuilt, I find this ray does the job quite well. The violet ray provides the situation with energy so you can transform past emotional hurts and wounds. When working with the violet ray, move the energy through you and imagine it extending out into your aura at least two feet in all directions.

THE LAW OF GIVING AND RECEIVING: COMPANION CLEANSES

Cleansing for Fulfillment

One of the ways you know you are out of alignment with this law is when you feel a sense of unfulfillment. Perhaps you are in a job that doesn't feel meaningful. Or maybe you have been "working" on a relationship for a long time. There are moments where you feel connected; however, the moments you feel alone, unsupported, and at times, uncared for can sometimes outweigh the positive ones. I see this sometimes when one person seems to put forth more energy, time, and thoughtfulness into a relationship than the other. When these kinds of situations go on for a long period of time, it can lead to buried feelings of resentment.

Yet time and time again, rather than process what they feel, I find people cover up their feelings with behaviors such as self-talk, sucking it up, or telling themselves they "don't care" or to just "let it go." Here is the thing: some people are set in their ways; they don't want to change. But this doesn't mean you can't change the energy. I once had a client who was wearing many hats in her office, and once she started working with the rays, she got the energy to let her boss know that they needed to hire additional staff members. Her boss agreed, and she felt more at peace with her job.

Clear Reactivity Sit up tall, and with your peace fingers, gently tap your chest area just below your shoulders, moving from one shoulder over to the other. This helps move stagnant energy in your heart center. Do this for about thirty seconds. Pause, take an inhale and an exhale, and move to the next step.

Look Inward *How I feel in my body right now is* . . . Inhale . . . exhale . . .

Now that I am cultivating energy, I feel . . . Inhale . . . exhale . . .

Making new and positive changes in this way makes me feel . . . Inhale . . . exhale . . .

Emit HUM three to five times as you release any reactions of unfulfillment.

Activate See it! Visualize the violet ray of light. See it streaming across the sky at sunset.

Nourish Feel it! Receive the energy of the violet ray fully and allow it to transform all hurts and resentment.

Surrender Say: *I allow fulfillment. I allow transformation. I allow abundance. I allow freedom.*

Ease Say: *I am fulfillment. I am worthy. I am transformation. I am mercy. I am free.*

Cleansing for Radiance

The rays of light are radiant. They beam with energy, illuminating your brilliance. Every living thing on the planet reflects radiance. Yet sometimes as a human being, you may feel your light is dimmed, and when this occurs, you can feel distant, insignificant, and depressed. You may then wonder, *What is my purpose? What am I supposed to be focusing on in my life?* These are all signs you are running low in vibration. These are great times to ask yourself what you are drawn to.

Some people are drawn to go outside more often or eager to relax on the beach, while others are looking for more structure and stimulation (like going back to school) in their lives. When you listen to your intuition and do what you are drawn to (for example, I would like to see the sunset), you cultivate radiant energy.

If the Law of Giving and Receiving could talk, it would say, *Go to the sunset. Sit under the tree. Join a club or cause.* Listen to the energy inside your body. *Notice, observe, allow, and receive* your energy in motion. Trust that the answers, direction, and guidance will come with movement. The key is that you are open and accessible to the signs and signals. Cleansing with the rays will help.

Clear Reactivity Place your right hand on top of your left shoulder as you sit in a comfortable seated position. Inhale through your nose (inflate your abdomen), and as you exhale through your nose, slowly pull your navel toward your spine (deflate your abdomen). Then switch arms, placing your left hand on your right shoulder. Again, take one slow inhale through your nose and exhale through your nose.

Look Inward *How I feel in my body right now is . . .* Inhale . . . exhale . . .

Being outdoors in nature makes me feel . . . Inhale . . . exhale . . .

Listening to my own guidance and intuition now makes me feel . . . Inhale . . . exhale . . .

Emit   HUM three to five times. Extend the last HUM so it is long.

Activate   See it! Visualize a violet ray in your mind's eye. Imagine it streaming through an image of radiance, like a tree, sunset, or meadow. What do you see?

Nourish   Feel it! Tune in to the violet ray, allowing it to soften your shoulders, face, heart, and body (similar to the way you might relax in the shower). May this feeling generously flow through you into Mother Earth.

Surrender   Say: *I allow trust. I allow admiration. I allow radiance. I allow freedom.*

Ease   Say: *I am understanding. I am radiance. I am transformation. I am free.*

Cleansing for Authenticity

When Amelia's sister told her she was fake, it just about broke her heart. After all, she had worked so hard to have a relationship with her sister. She spent time with her, bought her things, and took her places. Yet for whatever reason, her sister was pulling away, and the only explanation she got in return was this fake comment.

Here is the thing: when emotions are left unprocessed, you can come across to others as a little stiff or cold. While you may have a smile on your face or a positive attitude, some people (like Amelia's sister) are going to read between the lines. Yet what they don't understand is that when someone appears fake, chances are the energy of distrust (an old dynamic between you and this person) is present. This can happen when old wounds are not given permission to be fully processed. To show up as your authentic self, it is important to give not just to others but also to yourself. Otherwise, your efforts, like in the example above, won't last.

The Law of Giving and Receiving reminds us that giving and receiving are not about "doing." Giving and doing are not the same. When you give, think of it as an offering rather than an obligation.

You are offering your time, attention, energy, input, and invitation. When you give from a sense of obligation, it likely comes with a sense of effort. This law focuses on effortlessness.

I remember making a meal and putting it on the table for my three children. The girls started poking fun at each other and bantering. The energy did not feel good to me. The old me would have told them to knock it off and pushed myself through a tense dinner.

Since the girls were older, once I was finished with my meal, I left the table, went to my room, and read a book. I could hear the girls finishing their meal and having a respectful conversation. It was interesting to see how when I listened to my own energy and took myself out of the equation, the dynamic between the girls changed. The point being, I invited the girls to dinner and offered a meal. Had I pushed through something that didn't feel right, I would have done it out of "obligation." The Law of Giving and Receiving reminds us that less is more.

Clear Reactivity   Sit up tall in a comfortable seated position. Open your mouth wide, stretching your face. Release and repeat, opening your mouth wide and stretching it for five seconds. You might make the sound AHH while stretching your mouth open. After three times, relax, receive your breath, and move to step two.

Look Inward   *How I feel in my body right now is* . . . Inhale . . . exhale . . .

Offering my energy in this way makes me feel . . . Inhale . . . exhale . . .

Now that I am accessible and open to energy, I feel . . . Inhale . . . exhale . . .

Emit   HUM three to five times, tapping the roof of your mouth, and then do one long HUM at the end. Allow this HUM variation to lift, stir, and move any reactions contributing to stiffness.

Activate   See it! Visualize the violet ray streaming its vibrations of transformation, trust, and even forgiveness.

Nourish   Feel it! Receive the penetration of the violet ray similar to the way rain seeps into the earth. Offer this radiant energy to Mother Earth.

Surrender   Say: *I allow transformation. I allow vulnerability. I allow authenticity. I allow freedom.*

Ease   Say: *I am transformation. I am authenticity. I am accessible. I am free.*

Cleansing for Worthiness

Have you ever had a time when you felt bad about something? Perhaps the way something turned out was not what you intended. Initially you may have had high hopes or a positive attitude, but for whatever reason, it didn't last. As a result, you had to let go of the original idea of it all, only to be left with that sinking feeling of letting yourself down . . . again.

Here is the important thing about worth: it doesn't come from getting things right; it comes from moving through the moments when everything feels awful, bad, or wrong so when you find yourself in a similar situation, you can apply what you learned.

So if you try to keep it all together, to position everything perfectly, you will likely find the energy doesn't stick. In other words, the energy gains momentum, strength, durability, and true power by flowing in both directions: giving and receiving.

If the Law of Giving and Receiving could talk, it would tell you, *See "mistakes" as lessons of energy.* Don't run things so tightly that there is no room for error. This will clog up both giving and receiving. I always know when I am out of balance with this law when I start missing or forgetting appointments. This is a sign I am in doing mode, and as a result, I am more likely to miss important details, such as dates and times.

If you are feeling way out of balance with this law, allow the Cleanses and rays of light to bring the balance you need to be able to *notice, observe, allow, and receive* more freely.

Clear Reactivity   Get a nice cool glass of water and take a few small sips. Swallowing the water helps activate your vagus nerve. Notice how the water travels down your throat and into your tummy. Breathe in and out of your nose, inflating your abdomen area on the inhale and gently pulling your navel toward your spine on the exhale.

Look Inward   *How I feel in my body right now is* . . . Inhale . . . exhale . . .

Honoring my energy in this way makes me feel. . . Inhale . . . exhale . . .

Taking time to balance my energy now makes me feel. . . Inhale . . . exhale . . .

Emit   HUM three times as you release the need to "do."

Activate   See it! Imagine sitting by the ocean, taking in the scenery. Set your gaze on the horizon; notice the colors around you.

Nourish   Feel it! Tune in to the violet ray of light as you imagine your visualization. Let it touch you in some way. Give to yourself by honoring what you feel and receive calming benefits from this practice.

Surrender   Say: *I allow giving. I allow honoring. I allow receiving. I allow balance.*

Ease   Say: *I am giving. I am receiving. I am honoring. I am balance.*

MANIFESTING MESSAGE

One way to gently move yourself back into alignment with this law is by doing the following breathing exercise. Sit or stand up tall. Soften your eyes and notice your breath. Observe your inhalation and exhalation. Think of your inhale as receiving and your exhale as giving.

Now, ask your spirit, *Could I benefit from receiving or giving more?* Notice your bodily response, for example, if your inhale is longer than your exhale. Just notice. If you are inhaling more (after Cleansing), this may mean you could benefit from receiving more energy. If you are favoring your exhale (which can feel lower and shallower), you may benefit from giving (offering) energy (attention) to those around you or the planet. This could be as simple as picking up litter outside or helping a stranger by holding the door. There is no judgment here, just an opportunity to listen and learn how to balance your inner energy. If you could benefit from receiving more, try placing your palms together in front of your heart when you inhale and exhale. This can be a wonderful way to receive calm, presence, and self-love.

Affirmation: Giving and receiving come easily and naturally to me now.

CHAPTER 17

The Law of Rhythm

Tune in to this law to . . .
Increase energetic flow. Complete a cycle. Develop skills.

The Law of Rhythm shows us how everything in the universe is like a pendulum. It follows what Sir Isaac Newton's Third Law of Motion proves: for every action, there is an equal and opposite reaction. Whenever something swings in one direction, it will eventually return to the opposite direction. Should you choose to process your emotions and recognize your reactions along the way, when things do go back into balance, they will be better than before.

The Law of Rhythm is about cycles, transitions, and chapters coming to completion. Yet so often, old behaviors and thought patterns get repeated, which puts you in a reactive mode, and as a result, your flow gets interrupted. Over the years, I have found that reframing some of these thoughts can help. For example, rather than use the word "quit," reframe it as "completion" or "transition." Rather than "What if," say "What is." You may also reframe "What if" to "When." For example, rather than say, "What if they break up with me," instead say, "When this situation completes itself, I will feel . . ." Rather than say, "I quit my job," say, "I am in transition," or "That job came to completion."

Other words and phrases to look out for are "next" and "have to." When you are focused on what is next or what you have to do, you are no longer connected to the moment. Give yourself permission to complete something (energetically) before putting your attention on something else. While the world may be designed for multitasking, it doesn't really allow you to get into rhythm. Think of an artist painting. In order to create, manifest, and express what is inside of them onto the page, they get themselves in a bit of a zone. Imagine this artist answering their texts, emailing, or watching a movie at the same time. This would produce a very different energy.

Should things move out of balance, or rhythm, this law reminds you that everything will fall back into place. When, how, or in what way is out of your control. By consciously choosing to focus on the energy in action inside of you, you can work with the laws, and therefore, you will know that things will fall back to place in a better (less stressful) position than before. The point is that it is okay to be uncomfortable or a little out of sorts. Assume the Law of Rhythm is at work as long as you are moving energy. Work with the laws, not against them. Be a partner.

You are disconnected from this law when . . .

- You worry about the "What if?"
- You feel like you are managing the unknown.
- You think about what is "next" or are always trying to "figure things out."
- You need a concrete (rather than a flexible) plan or answer to move forward.
- You do something because you don't want to fall back (or regress to) the person you once were.
- You are fixated on wanting things a certain way.
- You spend a lot of time indoors or feel heavy or depressed.
- You feel anxious and therefore need to get prepared (have a plan B) "just in case."

You are connected to this law when . . .

- You go with the flow of life rather than resist it.
- You no longer view yourself as separate parts (such as "I used to be someone who drank too much").
- You are able to embrace and love all aspects of yourself without judgment.

- You feel whole and are able to be your authentic self in all situations (home, work, and so on).
- You listen to music or go for a walk out in nature.
- You are able to trust the subtle signs and synchronicities.
- You connect and open yourself up to others.
- You feel you have outgrown something and are no longer interested in old patterns (such as reactions).
- You feel guided and can see there are many pathways to take.
- You focus on energy (the way something feels inside) more than what people say or do.

CORRESPONDING RAY OF LIGHT: GOLD

The golden ray has many aspects. Some refer to it as the ray of Christ consciousness, while others emphasize this ray as Merkabah (light or spirit body). It is a ray of cosmic consciousness, capable of changing your DNA. This ray has the capacity to heal past wounds and traumas. In addition, it is a ray of activation, preparing you energetically for what is referred to as the New Earth. It is wonderful for transmuting negative energy, promoting truth and love, increasing your manifesting potential, and promoting clarity. When working with this ray of light, be sure to radiate it within and outside your physical body (beyond nine feet around). It is a powerful tool for protection and strength.

THE LAW OF RHYTHM: COMPANION CLEANSES

Cleansing for Centering

One of the most common ways people fall out of sync with the Law of Rhythm is by worrying extensively about others. It is difficult to connect to rhythm if you are preoccupied with preventing hurt or loss. Think of it like getting into your car, driving down the road, and realizing you forgot your wallet. You were on your way, but now you have to turn around, go back home, and retrieve it. Then you realize the time you had was lost, so you put off your errand for another day. This is what life looks like when you are out of rhythm.

You forget things more easily, get distracted, and move mindlessly through your day. In order to live harmoniously with the Law of Rhythm, as difficult as it may seem, ease up on your concerns about others. Otherwise, you may be giving lots of energy and attention to keeping the things you are worried about around. I know that is not what you want. Take some time to soften, center, and ground.

Clear Reactivity   Sit up tall and place your hands (one on top of the other) on your heart center. Breathe deeply in through your nose (inflating your abdomen) and out through your nose (deflating from navel to spine). Do this two or three times.

Look Inward   *How I feel in my body right now is* . . . Inhale . . . exhale . . .

When I allow rhythm and flow, I feel . . . Inhale . . . exhale . . .

Trusting the rhythm and flow inside me now makes me feel . . . Inhale . . . exhale . . .

Emit   HUM three to five times.

Activate   See it! Visualize the golden ray of light now in your mind's eye.

Nourish   Feel it! Receive these golden rays and allow them to expand your energy. May the individuals or situations that concern you also receive these rays now.

Surrender   Say: *I allow rhythm. I allow flow. I allow trust. I allow ease.*

Ease   Say: *I am rhythm. I am centered. I am balance. I am free.*

Cleansing for Harmony

Harmony happens when what you feel on the inside becomes a vibrational match for what you see on the outside. In a state of harmony, nothing feels forced. Instead, you are respecting the movement of energy. In other words, if you or someone you know feels sad, angry, or frustrated, you are detaching from the story and respecting the energy that is attempting to move through.

Now, if you are a parent, teacher, or a family member, you know all it takes is one person to be in a bad mood to impact the atmosphere. When the bad mood turns into a personality trait or attitude, it can put strain and tension on relationships. Trust that even personality traits can be transformed.

If the Law of Rhythm could talk, it would say, *Don't take things so personally, and for goodness' sake, quit trying to smooth things over. It is normal, natural, and necessarily for people to go through certain experiences to spiritually evolve.*

Notice when interfering begins to turn into enabling. It is a slippery slope. Remember, all healing comes with discomfort. When it may feel like things are getting extreme and people are disproportionately upset, turn to this law to have faith in the experience. Sometimes people have to go in the opposite direction to develop what they need to return to balance and harmony again.

Clear Reactivity   Sit up tall in a comfortable position. Relax your shoulders. Take a nice long inhale through your nose, inflating your abdominals for the count of four. Now, open your mouth wide, stick out your tongue, and let out a nice exhale, pressing your navel toward your spine. Do this two or three times.

Look Inward   *How I feel in my body right now is* . . . Inhale . . . exhale . . .

Respecting my energy makes me feel . . . Inhale . . . exhale . . .

Respecting others' energy makes me feel . . . Inhale . . . exhale . . .

Emit   HUM three to five times in a row.

Activate   See it! Visualize an image of harmony, rhythm, and flow, perhaps the golden color of the sun.

Nourish   Feel it! Allow these golden rays of light to penetrate your cells, aura, and energy field. Allow them to pass through you down into Mother Earth, releasing any trauma that's threaded through the DNA of planets, animals, and people.

Surrender   Say: *I allow strength. I allow harmony. I allow rhythm. I allow flow.*

Ease   Say: *I am strength. I am harmony. I am balance. I am free.*

Cleansing for Wholeness

Do you ever feel like you are separate, meaning the person you are at home is different from or separate from the one at work? Are you having a hard time integrating or being yourself in all situations? For example, you may feel confident at work, yet when it comes to raising children or navigating your love life, does your confidence begin to waiver? If so, tuning in to the gold ray in this Cleanse will help you transform old hurts (beliefs) and wounds that may be interfering with your ability to embody wholeness. For example, if you used to be a person who was unreliable and now you have changed your ways, there might be a part of you that still feels like people view you in the old way. While this might not be true, something inside of you still carries this feeling. This is because you haven't fully anchored your new, higher emotional energy yet.

Clear Reactivity   Sit or stand up tall with your feet hip-width apart so you feel nice and sturdy on the ground. Then take your arms behind you, interlace your hands (knuckles down to the floor), and stretch your chest and heart center. Hold this stretch for two or three breaths, release, and then move to the next step.

Look Inward   *How I feel in my body right now is . . .* Inhale . . . exhale . . .

Seeing myself as whole makes me feel . . . Inhale . . . exhale . . .

Now that all parts of myself are fully integrated, I feel . . . Inhale . . . exhale . . .

Emit   HUM three long exhalations.

Activate   See it! Visualize the whole, perhaps a circle, the sun, or a full moon.

Nourish   Feel it! Allow the gold ray of light to tingle down your spine into Mother Earth. Anchor the vibrations of harmony deep into the core of the planet.

Surrender   Say: *I allow integration. I allow wholeness. I allow unconditional love. I allow freedom.*

Ease   Say: *I am wholeness. I am unconditional love. I am enough. I am free.*

Cleansing for Presence

Presence is the practice of being in the here and now. One way to develop the practice is to learn to take your attention away from what is in front of you—situations, people, problems—and instead bring it to your body. Even a simple shift to noticing your feet on the floor or the way your hair touches your face strengthens your ability to be present. I encourage you to do this after your *"How I feel in my body now . . . "* statement or the soothing sound of the HUM. It won't be long before you notice the space this creates between your thoughts. Presence is the vibration of peace. Presence is the vibration of freedom. You are all of that and more.

Clear Reactivity   Sit up tall in a comfortable seated position. Press your palms together in front of your heart center, keeping your chin parallel to the earth. Keeping your chin in this position (rather than bowing your head) allows your breath to move fluidly through you. Inhale and exhale through your nose a few times.

Look Inward   *How I feel in my body right now is* . . . Inhale . . . exhale . . .

When I tune in to the here and now, I feel . . . Inhale . . . exhale . . .

When peace and freedom run through me, I feel . . . Inhale . . . exhale . . .

Emit   HUM three to five times.

Activate   See it! Imagine presence. How does it show up for you in your mind's eye? A picture of stillness, movement, or a color? Just notice.

Nourish   Feel it! Cultivate the gold ray of light into your image. Allow it to anchor presence through you and onto the planet now.

Surrender   Say: *I allow presence. I allow here and now. I allow expansion. I allow consciousness.*

Ease   Say: *I am expansion. I am presence. I am here and now. I am consciousness. I am free.*

MANIFESTING MESSAGE

Your final message:

Remember, one birthday candle can light all the other candles. Be sure to light your candle first and allow your light to spill over into the world. We are one (Law of Divine Oneness).

Be open and honest with yourself and others; your compensation will be that much sweeter (Law of Compensation).

You are not stuck (Law of Vibration). Things are shifting and changing for you, even when you can't see it (Law of Perpetual Transmuted Energy).

Focus more on the movement of energy (Law of Attraction) rather than what you want. Detach from outcome (Law of Detachment). Allow your inner movement to be the source of your own inspiration (Law of Inspired Action).

Know that what is happening in front of you is likely inside of you (Law of Correspondence).

Treat energy respectfully, and offer your energy to others freely, with no agenda or motive. Be sure to take time to receive to replenish yourself (Law of Giving and Receiving).

When things become too extreme or intense, aim for the opposite of what you are feeling; this is the direction for moving back to source (Law of Polarity).

Remember, everything in its rawest form is energy; therefore, don't get too attached to labels and meanings (Law of Relativity).

Know when things are out of sorts and you are having trouble finding your stride that things will fall back into place, most likely better than before, so long as you keep your energy in flow (Law of Rhythm).

The things you do or say have energy and ripple out into the world; keeping your energy in action will help you create peace and freedom (Law of Cause and Effect).

Your purpose is to cultivate energy so you can receive the love, guidance, and support around you. Let your spirit lead the way.

You are a multidimensional being. This means you have the capacity to move energy in such a way that you can create the life you desire. The practice of observing and noticing anchors you to the present moment. The practice of allowing and receiving gives you the means to access higher-dimensional frequencies (such as unconditional love, joy, abundance). One is not better than the other. They work in tandem, with each other and the Spiritual Laws of the Universe.

My hope is you will always choose to move energy first. See your emotions as the energy of your spiritual body. Nurture this aspect of yourself through the cleanses and rays of light. Practice regularly so you can discern the difference between a reaction and action. Cultivate your intuition so you can trust that your energy is in action, even when you can't see it. It is not about having but rather reconnecting and remembering you are pure love and light.

Affirmation: I am a creative being. I am energy in action.

Until next time, remember: your emotions matter; moving them matters more.

With love,

Sherianna

Acknowledgments

Thank you, Sounds True, for the energy you produce in the world and for your enthusiasm, support, and wisdom around this project. Thank you, Diana Ventimiglia and Alice Peck, two incredible editors. Alice, we did it again! And to Steve Harris, my literary agent, for your encouragement and guidance.

Thank you to my family. To my husband and best friend, Kiernan, for your support and love through this process. To my three daughters, Megan, Mikayla, and Makenzie, it is such an honor and privilege to be your mom. Thank you to Shannon Kaiser, Elizabeth Guarino, Bernie Ashman, Amy Leigh Mercree, and George Lizo for taking the time to endorse this book. Your support means the world to me. Thank you to Deborah Beauvais, founder of Dreamvisions 7 Radio Network, for your loving support.

Thank you to my mother, Judy, and my father, Larry; you both have been wonderful parents and grandparents. Finally, thank you to my readers, clients, and students for the opportunity to be both a teacher and student of energy.

Resources

Downloadable Rays of Light Charts can be found at sheriannaboyle.com/rays-of-light.

Continue Your Journey: Take part in the next Energy in Action Course.

Attend: A workshop or spiritual retreat.

Listen: Sherianna's *Just Ask Spirit* podcast

Visit: sheriannaboyle.com

References

CHAPTER 1

Marianne Williamson, *A Return to Love* (New York: Harper One, 1992).

Shosuke Suzuki, "Distinct Regions of the Striatum Underlying Effort, Movement Initiation, and Effort Discounting, *Nature Human Behavior* 5 (2021): 378–388, nature.com/articles/s41562 -020-00972-y.

CHAPTER 2

Tania Kotsos, "The Seven Universal Laws Explained," Mind Your Reality, mind-your-reality.com/seven_universal_laws.html.

William Hermanns, *Einstein and the Poet: In Search of the Cosmic Man* (Boston: Brandon Books, 1983).

Michael Miller, "Seven Amazing Facts About Emotions You Should Know," Six Seconds, February 19, 2018, 6seconds.org /2018/02/19/7-amazing-facts-emotions/.

Janie Pfeifer Watson, "90 Second Emotion Rule," Wholeness Healing Center, July 1, 2016, wholenesshealing.com/wholeness -healing-today/90-second-emotion-rule-2/.

Zoe Marae, Zoegraphy, zoeography.myshopify.com/pages/about-zoe.

Natalie Sian Glasson, *The Twelve Rays of Light* (Pembroke, Wales: Derwen Publishing, 2010), 78.

Natalie Sian Glasson, "Exploring the Twelve Rays of Light of the Creator," Sacred School of OmNa, October 5, 2018, omna.org /rays-light/.

Glenn Lewis, "The 13 Rays," Ascension Healing, May 11, 2020, ascensionhealing.co.nz/the-13-rays/.

Whitney Hopler, "Angel Colors: The Light Rays of Archangels," Learn Religions, April 29, 2019, learnreligions.com/angel-colors -light-rays-of-angels-123826.

Terry Gross, "A Physicist Explains Why Parallel Universes May Exist," Fresh Air, NPR, January 24, 2011, npr.org/2011/01/24 /132932268/a-physicist-explains-why-parallel-universes-may-exist.

CHAPTER 3

Trevor Haynes, "Dopamine, Smartphones, and You: A Battle for Your Time," Harvard University, May 1, 2018, sitn.hms.harvard .edu/flash/2018/dopamine-smartphones-battle-time/?web=1& wdLOR=c5DA354EF-A37C-8941-8394-D3BB23497677.

CHAPTER 4

Neuroscience News, "Increased Social Media Use Linked to Developing Depression," December 12, 2020, neurosciencenews .com/depression-social-media-17324/.

Neuroscience News, "How Sleep Helps to Process Emotions," May 13, 2022, neurosciencenews.com/sleep-emotion-processing-20578/.

The Council on Recovery, "How Does Spirituality Change the Brain?" May 7, 2019, councilonrecovery.org/how-does-spirituality-change -the-brain/.

CHAPTER 8

Sarah Regan, "Experts Explain What the Spiritual Law of Detachment Is and How to Use It," MindBodyGreen, September 10, 2021, mindbodygreen.com/articles/law-of-detachment/.

CHAPTER 12

Wallace D. Wattles, *The Science of Getting Rich* (Holyoke, MA: Elizabeth Towne Company, 1910).

About the Author

Sherianna Boyle is on a mission to get the world feeling again. She is the author of ten books, a professional speaker, adjunct psychology professor, certified professional coach, former school psychologist, and seasoned yoga instructor. She is the founder of Emotional Detox Coaching® and creator of the Cleanse Method.® Sherianna has been featured in over ninety articles and a presenter for renowned organizations, such as PESI® Behavioral and Mental Health Education, Kripalu Health & Yoga Center, 1440 Multiversity University, and more. Her book *The Four Gifts of Anxiety* was endorsed by the National Association of Mental Health. She works virtually using her energy-in-action techniques supporting clients worldwide. She is the host of the *Just Ask Spirit* podcast. Find her books, services, and weekly, live virtual membership at sheriannaboyle.com.

About Sounds True

Sounds True is a multimedia publisher whose mission is to inspire and support personal transformation and spiritual awakening. Founded in 1985 and located in Boulder, Colorado, we work with many of the leading spiritual teachers, thinkers, healers, and visionary artists of our time. We strive with every title to preserve the essential "living wisdom" of the author or artist. It is our goal to create products that not only provide information to a reader or listener but also embody the quality of a wisdom transmission.

For those seeking genuine transformation, Sounds True is your trusted partner. At SoundsTrue.com you will find a wealth of free resources to support your journey, including exclusive weekly audio interviews, free downloads, interactive learning tools, and other special savings on all our titles.

To learn more, please visit SoundsTrue.com/freegifts or call us toll-free at 800.333.9185.

sounds true
BOULDER, COLORADO